THE BOOKS OF
NAHUM AND ZEPHANIAH
A Study Manual

THE BOOKS OF
NAHUM AND ZEPHANIAH

A Study Manual

by

T. Miles Bennett

BAKER BOOK HOUSE
Grand Rapids, Michigan

PHOTOLITHOPRINTED BY CUSHING - MALLOY, INC.
ANN ARBOR, MICHIGAN, UNITED STATES OF AMERICA
1 9 6 8

To
BETH AND LINDA
delightful daughters
who filled a void in a
father's heart

PREFACE

In the providence of God Israel, during the eighth century B.C., had a quartet of prophets (Hosea, Amos, Micah, Isaiah) to instruct her in the way of righteousness. Also under God's providence, Israel had another quartet of spokesmen to give her moral guidance during much of the seventh century B.C. This group was composed of Nahum, Habakkuk, Zephaniah, and Jeremiah. The messages of two of these, Nahum and Zephaniah, are the concern of this commentary.

Although it is impossible to date with absolute certainty all of the ministries of either the eighth or seventh century prophets, it seems rather certain that some fifty to seventy-five years separated the two groups, when the voice of prophecy was silent. Isaiah was the last of the eighth century group and either Zephaniah or Jeremiah the first of the seventh century quartet. At least no names of great prophets are found in the Biblical record during this period. The lack of prophets at this time was due in part to the antagonistic attitude of the kings of Judah (esp. Manasseh and Amon) toward prophetic religion, and in part to the fact that no immediate danger threatened Jerusalem. Often it is some stirring political event in a nation's history that acts as an incentive to religious men to arouse the people to a sense of their sin and God's judgment. No such events occurred in Judah during the first half of the seventh century B.C.

However, outside of Judah events of tremendous importance and of vital concern to her national existence transpired. It was during the seventh century B.C. that the cruel and ferocious Assyrians reached the zenith of their power. And in the last quarter of the century this proud and merciless people experienced their decline and destruction. It is relative to this people that Nahum was divinely commissioned to speak. He is preeminently a prophet of one idea — the doom soon to descend upon Nineveh, the capital city of Assyria. Nahum was convinced that Jehovah though slow to anger would yet take vengeance on his adversaries. Therefore, he focused the light of God's moral government upon Nineveh and chanted the death-dirge of the world's greatest oppressor. God's judgment might be long deferred but it was certain, and it would be complete and final.

It is significant that Zephaniah's prophecy also is primarily concerned with God's judgment, although unlike Nahum he included his own people (Judah) in the judgment. Again, as with Nahum, events outside Judah vitally affected Zephaniah's message and his ministry. As early as approximately 650 B.C. the Scythians, a non-Semitic race of barbarians, swept in great hordes over western Asia striking terror into the hearts of all who heard of their savage cruelties. They later advanced southward along the Mediterranean coast as far as Egypt, and still later played a prominent part in the final destruction of Nineveh (612 B.C.). There is strong probability that Zephaniah considered the Scythians as the executioners of God's judgment upon his sinful countrymen and the surrounding nations, and saw in the threat of these mysterious hosts the harbinger of the day of Jehovah. On this day the fires of God's judgment would pass over Judah, Philistia, Moab and Ammon, Ethiopia, and Assyria consuming them as dry stubble.

It is at the point of the reality of the judgment of God upon nations and individuals that Nahum and Zephaniah make their most significant contributions. With both prophets judgment is one of the awe-inspiring inevitabilities of living in a moral world; that is, a world controlled by a moral God who demands of all men that they live according to his standard of righteousness and justice. In the sophisticated society of the modern world, where God if acknowledged at all is regarded as a "doting grandfather," and his judgment a myth of the past, the austere but clear words of these two seventh-century spokesmen for God should serve to remind all of the awesome actuality of Divine judgment.

CONTENTS

THE BOOK OF NAHUM

THE BOOK OF ZEPHANIAH

THE BOOK OF NAHUM

INTRODUCTION

Who was the prophet Nahum, whose very name may sound remote, unreal, strange to modern ears? About this prophet, the seventh in order of the twelve "minor" prophets in the English Bible, nothing is known except what can be gathered from the book bearing his name. One scanty reference (1:1) gives his name and the name of his place of birth. The name "Nahum" means "full of comfort" and is used nowhere else in the Old Testament. While the primary message of Nahum is the impending doom of Nineveh, a certain consequence of the fall of the Assyrian tyrant was relief for the oppressed of Judah. In this sense then the significance of his name corresponded to the effect of his message upon his hearers. The fall of Assyria would be hailed by every patriotic Israelite as the release of Judah from a hated foreign yoke.

Nahum is called the "Elkoshite" (1:1) which indicated that he was closely connected with a locality known as Elkosh. At least three locations have been suggested for this place: (1) Capernaum in Galilee, the name of which is a transliteration of two Hebrew words meaning "village of Nahum"; (2) Al-Kush, a place located some twenty-four miles north of Mosul (Nineveh); and (3) Elcesei, a village in southern Judah. In regard to the first view it cannot be maintained with certainty that Capernaum was named after the prophet. The second location is favored by those who insist that Nahum would have been unable to describe the doom of Nineveh in such graphic language unless he was an eyewitness to the events. But though the battles, both within and without the gates, are depicted with a degree of local knowledge, the historic allusions are not distinct, and there is no more reason to suppose that he had witnessed the destruction of Nineveh than that he had seen the siege of No-Amon (in Egypt), which he also described (see 3:8-10).

To raise question relative to the first two proposed locations for Elkosh is not to suggest that the third has been definitely es-

13

tablished. As a matter of fact, the place of Nahum's birth is still indefinite. It does appear more likely, however, that he was a native of the land of Palestine, although it is impossible to determine with finality the place of the prophet's birth. It may well have been that Nahum was born in Galilee, and later ministered in the south (Judah).

The date of Nahum's ministry is difficult to ascertain and can be established only within certain broad limits. Unfortunately and in contrast to many of the books of the prophets, the title verse (1:1) names no king or kings during whose reign the prophet labored (cf., e.g., Zeph. 1:1; Isa. 1:1).[1] The capital of Assyria is mentioned but when one recalls that the Assyrian empire was in existence for several centuries, the reference offers little help in dating the prophecy. It seems safe to assert that Nahum lived near the time of the fall of Nineveh in 612 B.C., but did he prophesy before, during, or after that event? Did he actually predict the fall of the city, or simply give a description of the event after it had transpired? Scholars are divided on the answers to these questions.

If one has no strong aversion to prediction as an integral part of Old Testament prophecy, Nahum's ministry can be established as falling somewhere within the rather wide limits of 663-612 B.C. The former date is the time of the fall of the Egyptian city of Thebes (No or No-Amon), mentioned in Nahum 3:8-10, and the latter is the time of the destruction of the Assyrian capital by the combined might of the Medes and Babylonians. Some scholars, feeling in Nahum's description of the fall of Thebes the force of a recent impression, have placed his ministry shortly after that event. Others, and for the same reason, that is, the vividness of the prophetic language, have placed his ministry shortly before the fall of Nineveh. This much is certain, the book presents Assyria as already or about to be invaded (cf. 3:13 ff.) by forces too great for resistance. Her populace showed signs of crumbling. Within as without, her doom was sealed. All of this would imply a state of hopelessness on the part of the people of the city of Nineveh. Such a

---

[1]For a discussion of the reliability of evidence found in the title verses, see the author's "Micah," *Shield Bible Study Outlines* (Grand Rapids: Baker Book House, 1968), p. 17.

condition existed in the life of this nation only during the last quarter of the seventh century B.C., the most likely time for Nahum's ministry.

The fact that the exact time of the prophet's ministry is unknown makes less difference perhaps with the Book of Nahum than with other books of the prophets. This is true for his message is directed exclusively at the certain overthrow of the wicked Assyrian. Such a message would have brought courage and comfort to Judah at whatever time it might have come in the history of Assyria, and particularly so at the height of her power and before signs of her destruction and decay were manifest to all.

The content of the book of Nahum is unique among the prophetical writing of the Old Testament. In this book one does not find a single word of condemnation against Israel and no call to repentance or reform. For the most part it contains a series of poems exulting over the fall of Nineveh, capital of the Assyrian Empire. Since the book has one supreme theme, the coming fate of Nineveh, it is complementary to the message of Jonah. This earlier prophet had preached repentance to Nineveh, and because her inhabitants had humbled themselves before God, the city was saved. But Assyria again lapsed into sin. Now it was Nahum's burden to predict the divine intention of her destruction. Nineveh's pride, cruelty, and idolatry were without limits. Too long the kings of Assyria had defied the God of heaven, placing the creator of the universe on a level with the gods of the surrounding nations. This blasphemy must cease, if not by repentance then by destruction. It was Nahum's lot to foretell the final downfall of the proud capital of the empire. In so doing he proclaimed the truth that God brings nations to an end if they fail to justify their existence.

It is impossible to understand the Book of Nahum without some knowledge of the world in which the prophet lived. Since his message is concerned solely with the overthrow of Nineveh, capital city of the Assyrian Empire, an acquaintance with the history of this people is prerequisite to an understanding of the vindicative spirit of Nahum's prophecy which some have called a "hymn of hate."

The name "Assyria" is derived from Asshur, a descendant of Shem (see Gen. 10:22). The country occupied the great region between the Tigris and Euphrates rivers, north of Babylonia. Its capital city was first located at Asshur and later at Nineveh. Asshur was the name of the supreme god of Assyria, and all wars and cruelties were ascribed to his commands. Cruelty was a much-vaunted characterisic of this people. As early as 1100 B.C. the Assyrian ruler Tiglath-pileser I, inscribing his victories on the rocks, boasted of his conquest of eighty-three kings and of how he littered the mountains with the corpses of their warriors. Some two hundred years later a distant descendant of Tiglath-pileser, Ashur-nasirpal II, proudly vaunted his savagery, telling how he flayed captive kings alive, dressed pillars with their skins, and walled up others alive before impaling them on stakes; how he burned boys and girls alive, put out eyes, cut off hands, feet, noses, and ears.

While the Israelites seemed to have escaped the full fury of the Assyrian atrocities, they certainly felt the oppressive hand of more than one Assyrian monarch. The first contact of Israel with Assyria occurred during the reign of Shalmaneser III (858-824 B.C.). In 854 B.C. Benhadad II of Syria and Ahab of Israel, along with the king of Hamath and nine other princes, entered into a confederacy for protection against Shalmaneser. Although the latter claimed to have slain some 20,000 men in a great victory, he apparently received a series of checks upon his ambitious plans of conquest. Nevertheless, some twelve years later he decisively defeated the usurper Hazael of Syria and forced Jehu, King of Israel, to pay him tribute.

During the next 118 years (744-626 B.C.) the nation Israel lived beneath the shadow of the might of six consecutive Assyrian rulers, namely, Tiglath-pileser II, Shalmaneser V, Sargon II, Sennacherib, Esarhaddon, and Ashurbanipal. The first of these was an organizer as well as a conqueror and began the policy of deporting conquered populations from one country to another. He also forced Menahem, King of Israel, to pay tribute and likely was responsible for the murder of Pekah and the elevation of Hoshea to his place as king of Israel (see II Kings 15). At this time many of the inhabitants of the northern kingdom were departed to Assyria.

Shalmaneser V, son and successor to Tiglath-pileser, took Hoshea captive to Assyria because of his conspiracy and began the siege of Samaria in 724 B.C. He died shortly thereafter and the siege was completed by Sargon II, who took the city in 721 B.C. and carried the tribes of the northern kingdom into captivity (see II Kings 17). Sargon was succeeded by Sennacherib, who after reducing Babylonia moved against Judah in 701 B.C. when its king (Hezekiah) revolted. During this campaign Sargon took captive some 200,000 prisoners. The city of Jerusalem was besieged but its capture was prevented by a pestilence that so decimated the invading army the siege was called off and the Assyrians returned home (cf. II Kings 19).

Sennacherib's son, and successor, Esarhaddon, captured Sidon, reduced Edom, Moab and Gaza to a state of dependency, and initiated a successful campaign against Egypt. According to the Biblical record (II Chron. 33:11) he took captive Manasseh, king of Judah, and carried him to Babylon, where for six months each year the Assyrian king held his court.

The last of the outstanding Assyrian monarchs was Ashurbanipal, whose reign began in 668 B.C. and continued for some forty-two years. Under his regency Assyrian dominion and power reached its zenith. It is likely that Nahum's ministry occurred during the closing years of his reign. While Judah was not included in the areas of Ashurbanipal's conquests, the world of his day trembled at his ferocious atrocities. Although he was a lover of learning and collected a great library of cuneiform tablets from which most of what is known of Babylonian and Assyrian literature has been derived, he was complacently cruel. He left on record how he tore off the lips and hands of kings, and how he compelled a prince to wear about his neck the decapitated head of his king. Following one of his many triumphs, Ashurbanipal was pulled along in a victory procession by three kings of Elam yoked to his chariot. On a sculpture now in the British Museum, he is represented sitting at a banquet with his queen, gazing on the head of a Chaldean king who had committed suicide.

Following Ashurbanipal's death in 626 B.C. the deterioration of his empire was swift and decisive. Although Assyrian records for the last twenty-five years of Nineveh's existence are missing, the details of her decline can be filled in from external sources. Rebellion within the empire and the growing menace of the Medes and the Chaldeans diminished Assyria's strength. Subject nations began to rebel against Assyrian domination, and in

17

614 B.C. Cyaxares, king of the Medes, invaded Assyria. He was repulsed but two years later the Assyrian capital of Nineveh fell before the combined assault of the Babylonians, Medes and Scythians.

All mankind rejoiced at the disappearance of this foul and horrible apparition which had afflicted the nations for more than five centuries. The Assyrians live before the world today upon their sculptures with their thick-set sensual figures, their calm settled ferocity, and their frightful nonchalance even while committing diabolical atrocities. They thought themselves impregnable in their capital city with its many (1200) towers and walls a hundred feet high, broad enough for three chariots to drive abreast on them. But they were swept away, and freed nations shouted for joy (see 3:19).

Such was the unprincipled power upon which Nahum, filled with an unshaken faith in the eternal righteousness of God, was commissioned to pronounce its doom. Is it any wonder that he said nothing about sins of his own people; rather, that the burden of his message was a fiery indignation, expressing the pent-up feeling of generations of suffering humanity? Even now one's righteous indignation is stirred to learn the history of human torture revealed in the triumphant note of miles of sculpture commemorating the horrid cruelty and craft of this once dominant race. Nahum's voice was not merely the voice of personal patriotism or vindictiveness but that of outraged human nature appealing for vengeance from God, as tyranny and inhuman cruelty forced their savage will on the weak and suffering of the human race.

The traditional view concerning the authorship of the Book of Nahum is that the entire content of the three chapters belongs to Nahum the Elkoshite (1:1). This view prevailed almost without challenge until the closing years of the nineteenth century, when questions were raised as to whether most of Chapter 1 belonged to the genuine oracles of Nahum. Such questions have persisted and today there is a widely prevalent view that the genuine work of Nahum consists of 1:11, 14; 2:1, 3-13; 3:1-19. To this material a later writer has prefixed a poem (1:2-10) which is an alphabetic acrostic, that is, each successive verse, or perhaps each line, begins with successive letters of the alphabet (Hebrew). According to this general view, 1:12, 13, 15, and 2:2

were also added to the genuine words of Nahum by a later writer, probably by the same one who prefixed the acrostic poem. The major obstacle to assigning the section (1:2-10) to the prophet is that the acrostic form is too artificial and mechanical for a writer of Nahum's vigor and freshness. While it may be true that the literary quality of this introductory poem is different from and perhaps inferior to the material of Chapters 2-3, the evidence is not sufficient to deny its authorship to Nahum.

Other theories have been suggested as to the composition of the Book of Nahum. In 1907 P. Haupt[2] advanced the idea that the book is a liturgy of four poems composed for the celebration of Nicanor's Day[3] in 161 B.C. According to Haupt two of these poems were written by an eye-witness of Nineveh's fall. P. Humbert[4] believed that the book was a prophetic liturgy composed after the fall of Nineveh, for the purpose of use at the Jewish New Year Festival in the autumn of 612 B.C. Alfred Haldar[5] has offered the theory that the book originated in an association of cult prophets who utilized ancient mythical and ritualistic themes to propagandize against Assyria and to inspire hopes of the national restoration of Judah. Suffice it to say that these theories are currently nothing more than theories, since the evidence adduced in their support still falls short of establishing their reliability.

From a superficial reading of the Book of Nahum one might conclude that it is devoid of religious value. Indeed the author has been classed with the nationalistic "false prophets" against whom Jeremiah and Micah waged relentless warfare (see esp. Jer. 23:28; Micah 3:5-8). But this is much too harsh a judgment. For while the very theme of Nahum's prophecy, the destruction of Nineveh, may preclude his reaching the spiritual heights of an Isaiah or a Jeremiah, there were certain fundamental prophetic truths which shaped his utterances. One of these is the sovereignty of God and his lordship over history. It

---

[2]"The Book of Nahum," *Journal of Biblical Literature,* 26 (1907), pp. 1-53.

[3]Nicanor was a general of Antiochus Epiphanes.

[4]"The Problem of the Book of Nahum," *Revue d'Histoire et de Philosophie religieuese,* 12 (1932), pp. 1-15.

[5]*Studies in the Book of Nahum* (Uppsala: A. B. Lundequistreka Bokhandeln, 1946), p. 6.

is a comfort to God's people in every age to be reminded that the eternal God is in active control of the affairs of his world. He controlled the history of mighty Assyria as well as insignificant Judah. His sovereign will is to hold sway to the ends of the earth. A second truth is that man lives in a moral universe and those who violate its laws must pay the penalty. The downfall of Nineveh was one of the most impressive examples in ancient history of the working out of God's laws of righteousness. Those who choose to live by the sword shall die by the sword (see Matt. 26:52). Nahum re-emphasized the truth, sounded by many of his predecessors in the prophetic office, that nations and empires founded on selfishness, treachery, force, and inhumanity cannot continue to exist. God will deal with them. To every such nation the prophet declared, "Behold, I am against thee, saith the Lord of hosts" (3:5a).

OUTLINE OF THE BOOK OF NAHUM

I. THE VERDICT OF GOD'S VENGEANCE ON NINE-
VEH (1:1-15)

Title Verse (1:1)

A. God's Character Is a Guarantee of Vengeance (1:2-6)
1. Jealous Vengeance (1:2)
2. Merciful Patience (1:3a)
3. Unlimited Power (1:3b-6)

B. God's Government Coincides with His Character (1:7-
15)
1. The Principle Stated (1:7-8)
2. The Principle Applied (1:9-15)

II. THE VISION OF GOD'S VENGEANCE ON NINEVEH
(2:1-13)

A. Destruction of the City (2:1-9)
1. The Siege (2:1-8)
2. The Sack (2:9)

B. Desolation of the City (2:10-13)
1. Description (2:10)
2. Derision (2:11-12)
3. Decree (2:13)

III. THE VINDICATION OF GOD'S VENGEANCE ON
NINEVEH (3:1-7)

A. The Vice of the City (3:1, 4)

B. The Result of the City's Vice — Judgment (3:2-3, 5-7)

IV. THE VERITY OF GOD'S VENGEANCE ON NINEVEH
(3:8-19)

A. The Lesson from No-Amon (8-13)

B. A Dirge of Doom (3:14-19)

I. THE VERDICT OF GOD'S VENGEANCE ON NINEVEH
(1:1-15)

Title Verse (1:1)

Nahum's oracles, as was customary in the prophetic writings (cf., e.g., Micah 1:1; Isa. 1:1; Ezek. 1:1), are introduced with a title verse or superscription. It is not necessary to insist that these words were penned by the very hand of Nahum but one must recognize that they do give witness to a very old tradition as to the author of the oracles. The double heading in this verse as well as use of the word "book" is unique to this prophet. Numerous attempts have been made to explain the presence of this double title, the majority of which are largely conjecture and should be treated as such.[1]

The burden of Ninveh. There is some uncertainty as to the meaning of the Hebrew word translated "burden." It is frequently found in the superscription of prophetic writings (see Hab. 1:1; Mal. 1:1), or at the beginning of independent prophetic oracles (see Isa. 13:1; Zech. 12:1). "Burden" is unquestionably the meaning in other usages of the word, where it denotes the burden carried by animals (see II Kings 5:17) and by men (see Jer. 17:21 f.) as well as the weight of sorrow and suffering (see Num. 11:11; Deut. 1:12). Others derive the term from the Hebrew verb which means *to lift* and translate it as "pronouncement," "utterance" or "oracle." The verb "to lift" may mean "to take up" in connection with a parable (see Isa. 37: 4), and an announcement of doom (see II Kings 9:25). It comes in effect to mean *to speak.* The choice between the two translations is difficult, but in view of the fact that in usage outside the prophetic titles the sense is primarily that of "burden," it is

---

[1]See e.g., Charles L. Taylor, Jr., *Nahum* "Interpreter's Bible," Vol. VI (Nashville: Abingdon Press, 1956), p. 957. For a contrary view, see W. A. Maier, *The Book of Nahum* (St. Louis: Concordia Publishing House, 1959), p. 148.

best to use that sense here. The interpretation of Nahum's prophecy as predictive of the *burden* which doomed Nineveh must bear is most appropriate for the message which follows.

Nineveh was one of the capital cities of Assyria, the first being Asshur located some fifty miles to the south. Its position relative to rivers and elevated places made it extremely difficult to overcome by direct assault. According to a tradition Nineveh finally fell in 612 B.C., only after a sudden rise of the Tigris River caused a section of the wall about the city to collapse. It was against this city, capital of a rapacious realm and characterized by sadistic cruelty and blood-stained magnificence that Nahum raised his inspired voice to foretell the "burden" of the destruction which divine justice demanded.

the book of the vision of Nahum the Elkoshite. While the use of the term "book" is found in no other superscriptions of this kind, there seems to be no valid reason for its deletion. Neither, however, does the presence of this word justify the explanation that Nahum simply penned his prophecies and never delivered them orally. "Vision" is a technical word, indicating that the source of the prophetic message was divine insight. The word may have originally denoted a literal beholding from its root *to see.* But it came to be used in a wider sense without any thought of actual physical sight. God's messenger might receive a "vision" through words or impressions which came from God. In this sense "vision" implies both revelation and inspiration. The prophet's name means "comfort" or "comforter" and is appropriate to his message when rightly understood. Nahum brought to his people no program of political expediency or plan of military conquest, but the promise of consolation which would be theirs with the overthrow of their hated oppressors, the Assyrians. The prophet is designated as the "Elkoshite," which apparently means that he was from a place named Elkosh, whose location is uncertain.[2]

A. GOD'S CHARACTER IS A GUARANTEE OF HIS VENGEANCE (1:2-6)

Many scholars hold the view that there is some evidence for an acrostic poem in Chapter 1, beginning with verse 2. An

---

[2]See Introduction, pp. 13 f.

acrostic is a literary device or form in which each verse begins with a successive letter of the Hebrew alphabet. There is considerable disagreement as to the length of this particular construction, since the acrostic is incomplete; that is, all twenty-two letters of the Hebrew alphabet are not included in the poem. Opinions as to its length range all the way from 1:2-7 to 1:2-23. Since the acrostic is incomplete numerous attempts have been made to complete it, resulting in textual emendations and reconstructions which cannot be justified.[3]

The theme of these verses (2-6) is the certainty and the severity of God's vengeance upon those who violate principles of righteousness in relationship to God and to one's fellow man. With cumulative repetition the prophet affirmed Jehovah's determination to take vengeance upon his enemies. Though he is slow to anger he will not acquit the guilty, but will hold them responsible and will bring them to judgment. Man is prone to lose sight of these moral truths and to conclude that because wickedness is permitted for a time it is condoned by God. This passage should serve to remind all that God's anger is ever against unrighteousness and that his judgment, though sometimes delayed, is certain.

1. Jealous Vengeance (1:2)

This verse lays the groundwork for the declaration of Jehovah's sentence against the offending city of Nineveh. It is the absolute righteousness of God that finally will demand the destruction of the Assyrian capital. Jehovah is mentioned three times in this opening verse and ten times in the first chapter. From the very beginning the prophet sought to set the certain doom of Nineveh in the right perspective; it was because of her religious and moral degeneracy that God was filled with wrath and vengeance against her. Therefore the prophet prefaced his message concerning this city with the restatement of the specific truth that God rebukes all who rise up against him in unrighteousness.

vs. 2. *Jehovah is a jealous God and avengeth.* The language employed in this verse is to be understood in the light of the fact that man can describe or characterize God only in terms of

---

[3]*Ibid.*, pp. 18f.

human language and experience. But the two usages must not be equated. Jealousy on the human plane involves the idea of being suspicious, distrustfully watchful, and fearful of rivalry. With God it is that eager zealousness which cannot tolerate any rival to the perfect love, fear, and trust that he demands from all mankind. The Old Testament picture of God as "jealous" involves a divine zeal which, unlike the idols of the heathen, cannot remain silent or passive in matters of righteousness and truth. "Avengeth" is closely allied to "jealous." But whereas jealousy involves intense emotional disturbance, vengeance is more volitional, active. While the vengeance of man expresses itself in retaliation, God's vengeance is retributive; that is, it is meted out to the recipient according to his just deserts as determined by the infallible judgment of God.

Jehovah avengeth and is full of wrath; Jehovah taketh vengeance . . . and reserveth wrath for his enemies. A second and a third time the Lord is presented as taking revenge. In all three instances the verb form is a participle, denoting that vengeance is a characteristic attribute. The unchanging God is an avenging Lord. As the God who avengeth, he is also "full of wrath," literally "lord" or master of heat; one who owns fury. Jehovah is the possessor of wrath; he controls divine anger and directs it wherever and against whomever he pleases, as he exacts full punishment. God's vengeance is directed against his "enemies" and his "adversaries," against whom he "reserveth wrath"; that is, lays it up or retains it, for his wrath is as eternal as himself. Nahum boldly asserted that, as the pages of human history are completed, one truth becomes clear: the Almighty reserves wrath for his enemies. This verse (2) then actually presents the theme of the entire book, namely, the certainty of God's vengeance upon the Assyrian capital because of the atrocities which she had committed.

2. Merciful Patience (1:3a)

vs. 3a. *Jehovah is slow to anger, and great in power, and will by no means clear the guilty.* The prophet now qualifies his repeated emphasis on God's vengeance. In order that no one receive an erroneous conception of divine wrath, it is further defined. His fury is not the unreasonable flaring up of the temper on the part of one who has not learned to control his passion, for "Jehovah is slow to anger." His anger is a perfectly controlled wrath; his fury a justified vengeance, resulting from a careful consideration and weighing of the whole matter. Man's anger against sin may be slow as the result of his lack of moral sensitivity. But God delays his wrath against sin and sinners because in his mercy he grants time for repentance. He is "not willing that any should perish" (II Peter 3:9). This delay however, should not be interpreted as weakness on God's part. Divine mercy is proof of strength, not of weakness. Only the weak are impetuous and impatient. Jehovah the God of power can wait. But this patient and powerful God "will by no means clear the guilty"; that is, he will neither treat them as innocent nor leave them guiltless. It may have seemed that Nineveh had gone unrebuked but Nahum protested that Jehovah would by no means permit her to escape the penalty of her iniquities. The fact that God had delayed for so long his stroke of judgment upon her made it all the more certain and imminent.

3. Unlimited Power (1:3b-6)

As further evidence of the certainty of God's judgment upon Nineveh, Nahum emphasized the power of Jehovah. His righteous character which demands that he punish the wicked city, is of no moment unless adequate power is available to execute judgment. The evidence of such power, suggested in 1:3a, is now firmly established. God's omnipotence is clearly seen in the natural world, in those elemental powers which man has ever been powerless to control.

vs. 3b. *Jehovah hath his way in the whirlwind and the storm.* These words do not merely describe God's approach in a theophany and "the convulsions of nature at the manifestation of divine presence." Nor do they necessarily imply that the overthrow of Nineveh will be marked by physical upheavals. Rather, the reference to whirlwind and storm is a poetical description suggesting the exalted power of Jehovah in its devastating punishment. The avenging God will sweep down upon the transgressors of Nineveh with the irresistible fury of a deadly tornado. The emphasis is upon the power of God, not his appearance.

the clouds are the dust of his feet. As man stirs up clouds of dust in his way upon the earth, so God in his exalted stride, approaching in the storm stirs up great clouds across the heavens. Again, the emphasis is upon his power.

vs. 4. *He rebuketh the sea, and maketh it dry, and drieth up all the rivers.* At the command of God the rivers and seas are dried up, as were the Jordan and the Red Sea (cf. Exod. 14: 21 f.; Josh. 3:7-17). But divine omnipotence cannot be limited to an historical reference; the all-powerful Jehovah can dry up any and all seas and rivers, and that by merely speaking ("rebuketh") to them (see Isa. 50:2).

Bashan languisheth, and Carmel; and the flower of Lebanon languisheth. God's avenging power is so great in its manifestations that not only do seas and rivers dry up, but green pastures and mountains wither and become barren. "Bashan" was the Transjordanic country which extended from Mount Hermon on the north to Gilead in the South. It was especially noted for its rich pasture lands (see Micah 7:14). "Carmel" is the fertile mountain that juts out into the Mediterranean Sea south of the Bay of Acre. Its beauty and productivity are proverbial (see Isa. 35:2; Jer. 50:19). "Lebanon" denotes the high mountains forming the northern boundary of Palestine famous for their cedars (see I Kings 5:6 ff.). These three areas were among the most fruitful of Palestine, the last to be affected by drought, but Jehovah's power is so penetrating that even these places droop and die before the manifestation of his omnipotence.

vs. 5. *The mountains quake at him, and the hills melt; and the earth is upheaved at his presence.* Even the mountains, regarded as ancient, permanent supports for the world (Job 9 5 f.) and as older than the world itself (Ps. 90:2) will collapse under his footsteps and move before his might. The hills, symbolic of permanency and stability, will also melt and disappear before the powerful presence of Jehovah. The word translated "upheaved" means *to heave* or *to lift up.* Perhaps the thought is that as God treads the earth in one place, it "heaves" or is "lifted up" in another, from the very weight of his majesty and might.

Yea, the world, and all that dwell therein. The sphere of Jehovah's mighty power includes not only the realm of nature, the inanimate universe, but also the domain of both beast and

28

man. Everything is within the circle of his sovereign might. The emphasis of these verses (3b-5) has been on the omnipotence of the Almighty God. In comparison with him the strongest forces of the universe are puny and helpless. How, then, can mighty Nineveh escape the full fury of his avenging wrath?

vs. 6. *Who can stand before his indignation? and . . . abide in the fierceness of his anger?* This verse draws a general conclusion from what has preceded. Having magnified the all-consuming power of Jehovah, Nahum now moved toward his theme, the certain destruction of Nineveh. In the light of God's hatred of sin, and in view of his awesome power which is adequate to punish sin, how can wicked nations hope to escape the ravages of his rage? This is the force of the rhetorical question which the prophet poses in the double interrogative: "Who can stand . . . ? and who can abide . . . ?" The answer is evident. No one can, not even the powerful and self-sufficient Assyrian. Jehovah's wrath is so hot that it consumes all who resist him.

his wrath is poured out like fire, and the rocks are broken asunder by him. The second half of this verse (6) continues the thought of the first half, the impossibility of standing before God's anger, which is "poured out like fire." Fire is an apt figure because of its destructiveness, sweep, and complete devastation (cf. Jer. 7:20; Ezek. 22:21). Once again the divine dynamic or omnipotence is emphasized. As God comes to execute justice and retribution the rocks, typical of durability and strength, shatter at his coming.

Having developed in implied fashion the thesis that God's judgment on Nineveh was certain because of his character, namely, his zeal to avenge wrong done against his absolute holiness and his unlimited though patient power, Nahum now seeks to present his thesis more explicitly. This was accomplished by showing that God consistently acts in accordance with his character.

B. GOD'S GOVERNMENT COINCIDES WITH HIS CHARACTER (1:7-15)

In verses 2-6 the prophet presented the character and nature of God which underlie his government of the world. Now Nahum shows how this principle operated as applied to God's friends (vs. 7) and his foes (vs. 8). These two verses (7-8) are theological and affirm general principles of divine government which make certain the overthrow of the tyrant and the security of those who trust God. In verses 9-15 Nahum makes specific application of this principle, first to Nineveh (Assyria) and then to Judah.

1. The Principle Stated (1:7-8)

vs. 7. *Jehovah is good, a stronghold in the day of trouble.* The word order of the Hebrew is stronger, "Good (is) Jehovah." Jehovah is declared to be *good;* not in the sense of capricious favor, but in terms of faithfulness in the administration of justice. Because of his faithfulness and righteousness Jehovah is the source of security for those who seek refuge in him. Nahum thus stressed the assurance of divine protection when he emphasized God's goodness. In the midst of dire warnings of doom and destruction, Jehovah offers to his own the security which protecting ramparts provide the soldier. God is the incomparable refuge for his own in "the day of trouble." "A Mighty Fortress is our God, a bulwark never failing," is the way Martin Luther put it in his Reformation hymn. In his reference to God as a "stronghold," Nahum likely intended a contrast with the walls of Nineveh, in which the Assyrian trusted. Those walls appeared impregnable, but they would provide no protection in the day of God's visitation in judgment upon those within them. In contrast Jehovah is a "stronghold" to those who look to him in faith.

he knoweth them that take refuge in him. The Hebrew verb for *know* involves more than an intellectual awareness of, or a mere theoretical acquaintance with; it is more personal and intimate. For example in the statement, "And the man *knew* Eve his wife; and she conceived, and bare Cain" (Gen. 4:1), the first verb used is a form of the Hebrew "to know." To say that God *knows* means that he is vitally interested in and has loving concern for the person or persons known (cf. Ps. 1:6). This involves his uninterrupted concern for their welfare as well as for the direction of their lives. Such knowing is, as the Hebrew participle indicates, a characteristic trait of God — he is "all the time knowing," and it is reserved for those who trust in him, who seek refuge only in him. Surely these words brought comfort to Judah in her long day of trouble!

vs. 8. *But with an overwhelming flood he will make a full end of her place.* After presenting the general principle that God, whose actions always coincide with his character, has an intimate concern for those who trust him, Nahum next presented the contrasting truth that God will bring ultimate destruction upon his foes. God's goodness does not change the fact that he is and ever remains a God of vengeance against his enemies. Devastation by flood is frequently mentioned in the Old Testament, sometimes as literal (e.g., Gen. 7) and again figuratively (e.g., Isa. 8:7). Both interpretations have been proposed for this verse, but the former is preferable. Greek tradition is in agreement with the interpretation of an actual flood. Diodorus Siculus, a historian living about the time of Christ related that the Euphrates (incorrectly for Tigris) flooded its banks, causing more than two miles of Nineveh's wall to collapse allowing the enemy's entrance into the city. Furthermore, Nahum spoke of the flooding of the city in two additional passages: "The gates of the rivers are opened, and the palace is dissolved" (2:6), "Nineveh is like a pool of water" (2:8). By means of flood then, God "will make a full end of her place." "Her place" properly refers to Nineveh though some translations substitute "his adversaries" (cf. RSV). To the argument that there has been no mention of Nineveh thus far in the prophecy, hence the suffix "her" is without antecedent, suffice it to say that the title in verse one makes clear reference to Nineveh. "To make a full end" is to annihilate, to completely destroy. This was the fate of the Assyrian capital, and it is said that when Alexander the Great centuries later passed over the place formerly occupied by Nineveh, he was unaware that a great city had ever occupied the spot.

and will pursue his enemies into darkness. The subject of this clause is Jehovah. The meaning is either that God will relentlessly seek out his enemies, even if they attempt to escape into the darkness, or that he (Jehovah) will drive them out of the light into the darkness where they must ultimately perish.

It is clear from these verses (2-8) that it is Jehovah's character or nature to visit the full weight of his wrath upon his foes, a visitation which always results in their destruction. Conversely, it is his nature to manifest an intimate concern for those who are rightly related to him, a concern which always works to their good. Nahum now turns to make specific application of these principles, particularly to Nineveh but also to Judah.

2. The Principle Applied (1:9-15)

With verse 9 there is an abrupt change as the prophet's words are leveled directly at the Ninevites. The statements which follow are made more difficult of interpretation because the speaker, with fiery eloquence surges back and forth, first to Nineveh, then to Judah. Many commentators[4] have forsaken both caution and common sense in dealing with these verses in their efforts to force modern thought-patterns of unity, coherence, consecutiveness, and progression upon an ancient literature produced by a people whose psychology was vastly different from ours. There is a very close connection between this section and the preceding one. The same theme, the certainty and severity of God's vengeance upon his enemies, is pursued, and two thoughts previously noticed are further developed, namely, the annihilation of Assyria and the consolation of Judah.

vs. 9. *What do ye devise against Jehovah?* The question is directed to the Assyrian, "Whom do you think God is?" It is asked in derision as the prophet mockingly inquires what God's enemies (Assyria) can do in view of his decree of doom, and of his declared intention to "make a full end" (cf. vs. 8).

affliction shall not rise up a second time. The punishment that Jehovah will mete out to Assyria will be such that he will not need to repeat it. His blow upon her will be irreparable. A different but related interpretation of this verse has the question directed to Judah in the sense, "What makes you doubt?" Punishment of Assyria is certain. You will be no more overrun as in the past. The reference is perhaps made to the invasion of Judah by Sennacherib (see Isa. 37).

vs. 10. *For entangled like thorns, and drunken as with their drink, they are consumed utterly as dry stubble.* This verse has been described as "one of the most difficult in the entire

---

[4]For examples of these, see W. A. Maier, *op. cit.*, pp. 184 ff.

book." This writer agrees; nevertheless, its import is reasonably clear, the destruction of Nineveh will be full and final. Dry thorn cuttings were a common fuel in Palestine. A second highly combustible material, also popular as a fuel, was the dry straw and stubble of the threshing floor. Under the all-consuming fire of God's judgment Nineveh will be as utterly consumed as these fast-burning fuels. Though the Assyrian be soaked in wine, he shall burn as the driest of fuels in the day of Jehovah's wrath. Nineveh, ever carnal and careless, will be completely consumed. "Drunken with their drink" may refer to the arrogant independence of the Assyrians and their defiant disdain of any danger from without. It may also refer to the complete impotence of the Assyrian soldiers in the time of God's judgment. They shall be as helpless and halting as thoroughly drunken men. It is of interest to note that according to tradition Nineveh was taken while its defenders were indulging in riotous drinking.

vs. 11. *There is one gone forth out of thee.* Nineveh is again addressed. One has gone forth from her, that is, at her direction, with her support. Numerous identifications have been advanced for the one sent out by Nineveh. Some see a collective usage, referring to all the Assyrian monarchs who had gone out or would go out to oppress the people of God. Majority opinion, however, favors the view that "one" refers to Sennacherib, who was the most aggressive foe of Judah, invading her during the reign of King Hezekiah (see II Kings 18).

that deviseth evil against Jehovah, that counselleth wickedness. The prophet charged Nineveh not alone with sending out one who had been guilty of brutal destruction, but who had plotted evil against Jehovah himself. The invasions led by this general were not only against the Israelites, but since they were in covenant relationship with Jehovah, the invasions were seen as directed against Jehovah himself. Back of the overt act of invasion, there were schemings and plottings of wickedness and worthlessness by this "wicked counsellor" (Sennacherib).

vs. 12. *Thus saith Jehovah.* This is the only usage of this common prophetic formula (see, e.g., Isa. 45:1; Jer. 17:5) in the entire book of Nahum. Its presence is not merely introductory; rather it served to validate the prophet's message. Since this word of judgment was from God and not man, its fulfilment was certain. Furthermore, it was the prophet's declaration that he was God's spokesman, therefore, all men were obligated to heed what he said.

though they be in full strength, and . . . many, so shall they be cut down, and he shall pass away. It is difficult to determine whether Nahum here refers to Sennacherib's invasion (vs. 11) of Judah in 701 B.C. or to a later invasion of Nineveh herself. At any rate the emphasis is upon the fact that the Assyrian's strength will be cut off.

Though I have afflicted thee, I will afflict thee no more. These words were addressed to Judah not Nineveh, and for the purpose of consolation. Encouragement had come to Judah from the announcement that the strength of the Assyrian was about to be destroyed (vs. 11). God had afflicted Judah by means of the Assyrian invasion of 701 B.C. and the subsequent tyranny of the heathen tyrant. Now he was prepared to pledge the cessation of all sufferings which originate in Nineveh, "I will afflict thee no more." What comfort and consolation these words must have brought to Judah!

vs. 13. *And now will I break his yoke from off thee, and will burst thy bonds in sunder.* As further assurance that Judah would no more suffer affliction from Assyria, God made a two-fold promise: first, to break the Assyrian yoke, and second to burst the bonds with which Assyria held Judah in subjection. Judah was a vassal kingdom, paying tribute to Assyria (cf. II Kings 18:14), but Jehovah had determined to liberate his people. The yoke of Assyrian oppression and domination was to be broken, and the fetters which had rendered Judah helpless were to be torn apart by Jehovah himself (cf. Isa. 14:25; Jer. 30:8).

vs. 14. *And Jehovah hath given commandment concerning thee.* To the promise of release for Judah the prophet added a series of direct threats against Nineveh. These threats came as a commandment or decree from Jehovah. So again, as in verse twelve, Nahum spoke in the capacity of a divine messenger, charged with pronouncing a divine sentence on a doomed city. The predictions to follow were not the futile threats of fallible man, but the immutable decrees of an infallible God.

that no more of thy name be sown. Jehovah had decreed that Nineveh, the Assyrian capital and representative of the empire should have no progeny, her national life should cease completely. Not only would she be destroyed but she would become extinct. From inscriptional evidence it seems that Assyrian kings were especially concerned that their names be perpetuated. Ashurbanipal concluded his annals with the request that his successor preserve his name on a building inscription and warned that anyone who removed it would be cursed by the eleven most powerful gods in the Assyrian pantheon.

out of the house of thy gods will I cut off the graven image and the molten image. These words serve to emphasize the religious nature of the conflict (between Jehovah and Assyria) and also to point out the triumph of Judah's God over the gods of Nineveh. The Assyrians not only bestowed lavish attention upon their temples, which abounded particularly in stone figures and sculptured bas-reliefs, but it was also customary for them to desecrate the temples and altars of their conquered foes, and to deport their idols, for the purpose of emphasizing the supremacy of the gods worshiped at the Assyrian shrines. Now this haughty people was to experience the same desecration that had been inflicted upon others. They had totally destroyed the temples of other nations; now their own would serve as fuel for fire. They had shown utter contempt for the gods of other peoples (cf. Isa. 36:13-20); now their own would be cut down in a graphic demonstration of their absolute impotence.

I will make thy grave; for thou art vile. These words of warning made it plain that Nineveh was not merely to be temporarily incapacitated; her lot was death and burial. Jehovah was making a "full end of her place" (1:8 f.). Jehovah had rejected Nineveh for she was "vile," literally, *light,* lacking worth (moral) and weight. When weighed in the balances of divine righteousness, Nineveh was found "vile," light, wanting (see the related thought in the Aramaic of Dan. 5:27, "weighed in the balances and . . . found wanting").

vs. 15. It is not clear why this verse has been made the first verse of Chapter 2 in the Hebrew. Its close relationship with the first chapter seems natural. Nahum has announced a number of threats against Nineveh. He is so confident of their fulfilment that he has a messenger announce it as done even before the events actually occur.

Behold, upon the mountains the feet of him that bringeth good tidings, that publisheth peace. The prophet portrays the joy with which Judah will receive the news of the overthrow of Nineveh. As the consequence of this overthrow, there will be relief for the oppressed people of God. The arrival of this good news is declared in picturesque fashion, a messenger comes running across the mountains. The messenger brings good tidings of peace. Nineveh, "the tyrant on the Tigris," has fallen. Perhaps it was because news must of necessity come to Jerusalem by mountain roads that the "good tidings" were announced by the prophet in this form (cf. Isa. 52:7).

Keep thy feasts, O Judah, perform thy vows. Either the herald or the prophet urged the people to express gratitude for their deliverance at the hand of Jehovah. Now that the oppressor was no more, Jerusalem was to return to normal religious life, keeping the feast and performing the vows — vows made to God during the time of trial.

for the wicked one shall no more pass through thee; he is utterly cut off. The reason for the proclamation of peace is that Jehovah has destroyed the "wicked one." This wicked one is most likely Assyria personified, rather than reference to a particular king or succession of kings over Assyria. Judah can anticipate a time of peace, progress, and prosperity, a time of uninterrupted devotion to her God, now that the cruel oppressor has been annihilated.

Thus Nahum deals in chapter one with the overthrow of Nineveh in an introductory and general manner. He has presented his theme against the background of the character and nature of Jehovah and the oppressed people of Judah. In the remaining chapters (2) he sets forth the accomplishment of Nineveh's destruction with a clarity and forcefulness, unsurpassed among the prophets.

II. THE VISION OF GOD'S VENGEANCE ON NINEVEH
(2:1-13)

Nahum has foretold in somewhat general terms the utter destruction of Nineveh. Now he comes to fill in some of the details of the extinction of that ancient citadel of crime. As one writer has suggested, "The scene changes from the presence and awful arsenal of the Almighty to the historical consummation of His vengeance."[1] Even though the fall of the city was an anticipated event it is pictured in vivid color and some gory detail. But how accurate was Nahum's description? Is there a close correspondence to what actually happened when the city fell in 612 B.C.? Unfortunately only a scanty record in contemporary literature has been discovered. The Babylonian Tablet, discovered by C. J. Gadd of the British Museum, is the most reliable source of information currently available. It contains the date of the city's fall, and supplies some information concerning the fall of certain other Assyrian strongholds. It is not necessary to demand that Nahum's account contain every detail that actually transpired at the fall of Nineveh. Certainly the prophet was familiar with the predominant weapons and methods of warfare in his day, and he gave us a typical or representative picture of such, as he vividly described the irresistible attack of an army on Nineveh.

A. DESTRUCTION OF THE CITY (2:1-9)

1. The Siege (2:1-8)

vs. 1. *He that dasheth in pieces is come up against thee.* These words announce the approach of an advancing army. "Is come up" is a technical term used of hostile military operations (see I Sam. 7:7; I Kings 20:22; Isa. 7:1). The Hebrew verb is in the perfect tense, the tense used to describe action already completed. Doubtless this is the so-called "prophetic perfect," used by the prophets to describe future actions of which they

---

[1]G. A. Smith, *The Book of the Twelve Prophets*, Vol. II, (New York: Harper & Brothers, 1928), p. 95.

were so certain that they spoke of them as having already occurred. "He that dasheth in pieces" is the rendering of a single Hebrew word (participle in form), variously translated as "hammerer," "shatterer," and "disperser." The latter meaning has much in its favor, not only in terms of its frequent use in this sense (see II Sam. 22:15; Isa. 24:1; Jer. 18:17), but perhaps from the standpoint of retributive justice as well. Assyria was the ancient nation who began the practice of carrying off, or "dispersing," large segments of the population of conquered countries. The cities or countries left vacant were repopulated with people from other parts of the empire (cf. II Kings 17: 23 ff.). This was done for the purpose of rendering the conquered nations powerless. Now the great "disperser" was herself to be *dispersed,* and hence rendered impotent. But who was this "scatterer"? Was he human or divine? Perhaps the former, though, of course, Nahum saw Jehovah as the causative force in the dispersion. As to the identity of the "disperser," why should the interpreter speak when the prophet was silent?

keep the fortress, watch the way, make thy loins strong, fortify thy power mightily. Because the "disperser" had come up, Nineveh, besieged few times in its long history, would have to do what its proud and powerful armies had often forced other cities to do. The cry goes out, "Man the ramparts," guard your munitions and fortifications; "Watch the way" (road), keep a sharp lookout on all the highways, leading into the city; "Make the loins strong," muster all the courage possible, you will have need of it; "Fortify your power mightily," make use of every means possible to present a strong, solid front. The four verbs used are a form (infinitive absolute) which expresses the force of the word with maximum emphasis. These four commands have been understood in different ways: Some view them as the ironical words of the prophet to the city, "Go ahead and prepare, take every precaution possible. All will be futile, for you are doomed." Others consider these words as the frenzied cries of the inhabitants of the doomed city. And still others view them as the terse commands of military officials desperately calling upon citizenry and soldiers alike to repel the attackers. The first of these views seems more in keeping with the spirit of vengeance found throughout the prophecy.

vs. 2. Since this verse seems to "break the continuity" between verses one and three, numerous suggestions have been advanced to solve the purported problem of its present position. George Adam Smith[2] proposed that this verse should close the previous chapter and in his own translation placed it following 1:15. Another group of interpreters looks upon 2:2, along with 1:10, 12, 13, 15, as a series of marginal notes[3] added by a post-exilic editor, probably the same one who added the acrostic poem of 1:2-10. But is the verse out of place? Does lack of continuity prove the presence of material by another author? Did the Hebrew prophets always speak in logically developed fashion? Rather, are not their messages characterized by a rapid shifting from one thought or theme to another? And when spoken under the white heat of intense passion, as Nahum spoke, this lack of logical progression would be all the more evident. But wherein is the content of verse 2 so illogical as related to the preceding and following verses? What could be more logical than for Nahum, after announcing the advance of an invader upon Nineveh (vs. 1), to give the reason for his coming (vs. 2), and then to return to the description of the invasion or siege (vs. 3)?

For Jehovah restoreth the excellency of Jacob, as the excellency of Israel. Here is the reason for the enemy's besieging Nineveh. The Lord had seemed to forsake his people when he allowed the Assyrian to invade and ravage their land. But he was still jealous for them and would avenge the wrongs done them. Therefore God had summoned the "disperser" to move against Nineveh that he might "restore the excellency of Jacob." The "excellency of Jacob" is that in which Jacob justly glorified, all the privileges and responsibilities with which God had blessed his people. "Jacob" and "Israel" are taken by some as meaning the kingdoms of Judah and Israel respectively, although the meaning is less than clear when such is done. Perhaps both words stand for the whole people. Or better still, since the name "Jacob" was the name given by man and "Israel" that conferred by God, correspondingly the "excellency of Israel" is something higher and more glorious than the "excellency of Jacob."

---

[2]*Op. cit.*, pp. 93 f.
[3]Charles L. Taylor, *op. cit.*, p. 960.

for the emptiers have emptied them out, and destroyed their vine branches. These words express the reason why God would restore his people; their enemies had inflicted the full measure of punishment. They also suggest the reason for Nineveh's fate. Although the Assyrians were God's instrument in punishing his people, they too are to feel the fury of God's wrath because of their cruel, ferocious pride. They had plundered God's people and "destroyed their vine branches." The people of Israel are often pictured as God's vineyard (cf. Isa. 5; Ps. 80:8 ff.). The figure need not be pressed too far by an attempt to make the "destroyed vine branches" stand for the cities of Judah which had been destroyed by the Assyrians. But Judah's pitiable plight is significantly symbolized by the picture of a vine, despoiled of fruit and branches broken, with little more than the trunk remaining.

vs. 3. As Nahum returns to his picture of the besieging army, one need not expect him to fill in every detail of the assault upon Nineveh. Rather, brief and rapid flashes of the future pass before his mind's eye.

The shield of his mighty men is made red, the valiant men are in scarlet. The antecedent of the pronoun in "*his* mighty men" has been variously identified. Some hold that the reference is to the unnamed Assyrian king, but the vagueness of this monarch's introduction makes this view seem unlikely. Others point to Jehovah himself as the one to whom the "mighty men" belong. Although the attitude by which Jehovah calls the forces attacking Assyria his own is not without parallel (cf. Isa. 13:3 f.), the language of the context seems far better suited to the one "that dasheth in pieces" (cf. vs. 1) as the one to whom the "mighty men" belong. It is his army that is pictured in "exquisite battle array," clothed in scarlet and carrying shields covered with skins dyed red.

the chariots flash with steel in the day of his preparation. More literally, "the chariots are with fire of steel." The reference is doubtless to the attacker's metal-covered chariots which fairly blazed in the Assyrian sun. "Day of *his* preparation" refers not to God but to the preparation of the enemies of Assyria.

And the cypress spears are brandished. Although "spears" is missing in the Hebrew the reading is correct. Spear shafts were frequently made from cypress, highly prized for its durability. These spears were "brandished," or waved, by men eager for battle.

vs. 4. From the picture of preparation for battle, Nahum turns to a description of the battle (siege) itself. This verse seems to refer to the fighting in the suburbs of the city which took place before the walls were assaulted. Again, as in verses 1 and 3, the language is terse, swift, and highly charged with action and emotion.

The chariots rage in the streets . . . they run like the lightning. For Nahum the most impressive thing about the invaders was their charging chariots. These "wagons of war" dashing madly through the "broad ways" struck fear into the hearts of the Ninevites. As the prophet beheld the chariots gleaming in the sunlight and bolting from one place of attack to another, he compared them to flaming torches and strokes of lightning.

vs. 5. In this verse attention is focused on the fight for the very walls of the city of Nineveh. Older versions and commentators generally take as the subject of the verbs of this verse the Assyrians (or their king), while newer versions and more recent commentators consider the invaders (or their leader) as the subject. To this writer the logical progression of thought to a proper climax favors the latter interpretation.

He remembereth his nobles: they stumble in their march. Remember in the sense of calls upon "his nobles," that is, his best military units, in this case those trained to assault the walls of a city. These specialized troops, in their haste and zeal to achieve their objective, "stumble" or better, crowd against or jostle one another.

and the mantelet is prepared. "The defense shall be prepared" (KJV) is poorly rendered. Most other translations render the Hebrew (*cover, covering*) as "mantelet," which denotes some kind of shelter or covering used by the besiegers as they operated various kinds of siege machinery.

vs. 6. The battle raged. The siege was pressed. The cunning besieger, employing every tactic known to ancient warfare, finally made use of one of the very resources upon which Nineveh had depended for her own protection — the rivers.

The gates of the rivers are opened. Three rivers, the Tigris, Tebiltu, and the Khoser, flowed either adjacent to or transversed

41

the city of Nineveh. In addition there seemed to have been a network of canals and defensive moats. In conjunction with these canals, moats, and at least one of the rivers, dams and sluices were constructed to aid in control of their waters. It is highly probable, then, that the reference to "gates of the rivers" refers to the opening of sluice or dam gates, releasing large volumes of water of sufficient force to breach the city walls and thus allow the enemy to enter. Indeed the Greek historian Diodorus Siculus has written how the river became "an enemy to the city" during a siege by the foe. While at present archaeological evidence has not established conclusively that flood waters played a vital part in the destruction of Nineveh in 612 B.C., one may well suppose that Diodorus' account was based upon an ancient local tradition concerning her destruction.

and the palace is dissolved. If flood waters did play an important part in the downfall of Nineveh (see above), the meaning here is that the very foundation of the Palace was dissolved, or at least made easy of overthrow by the waters. Otherwise the interpretation is that the palace was dissolved with terror and consternation. The heart of king and princes melted when they heard of the successful assault upon the walls of the capital city by the enemy.

vs. 7. *And it is decreed.* This is one translation of a single Hebrew word (*huzzab*) whose meaning still remains a mystery. Various interpretations of the Hebrew original have been proposed. Some, as here, translate it as a verb, "It is decreed," or "There was a stand made." Others consider it as a noun, "mistress" (RSV). Still others consider the word a proper name (KJV), either of an Assyrian queen or goddess or a name personifying Nineveh itself. The feminine gender is indicated by the feminine ending of the Hebrew verb used with the word. Probably the word is best explained as a proper noun designating either the Assyrian queen, although no queen by this name is known to history, or more likely Nineveh personified, although this is the only Biblical usage of the word.

she is uncovered, she is carried away. The uncovering or stripping indicates that Nineveh was at the mercy of her captors. She was subjected to an indignity customarily done to captive people, parading naked before their conquerors (cf. Isa. 47:2 f.), as she was "carried away" into captivity. The Assyrians had frequently stripped their captives; now Nineveh would receive the same harsh treatment that she had meted out to others.

and her handmaids moan as with the voice of doves, beating upon their breasts. If the "handmaids" of the queen are meant, the interpretation is obvious: they mourn like doves (from their cooing or mournful sound) because their mistress is taken away captive. If the reference is to the handmaidens of Nineveh personified, then the language is figurative: just as the queen's maids would mourn her going into captivity, so would the "handmaids" of the queenly city of Nineveh mourn her conquest by the enemy. "Beating upon the breasts" (lit. *heart*) was an action expressive of intense, deep sorrow.

vs. 8. *But Nineveh hath been from of old like a pool of water.* Nineveh is described as from her beginning "like a pool of water," that is, both wealth and population had been continually replenished, just as new waters flow into a pool. Throughout her existence this city had been constantly swelled, like a pool of water, by the constant influx of wealth and people.

Yet they flee away. Stand, stand, they cry; but none looketh back. Nineveh's multitudinous population is of no avail in the day of her siege. They flee in the unchecked haste of utter panic, seeking safety in headlong flight. In the midst of this wild confusion and disorder, Nahum heard the frenzied cries, perhaps of an army officer or a leader of defense, "Stand!" "Halt!" But no one heeded. None so much as looked back. Nineveh's defeat was complete. God had made "a full end" (see 1:8 f.) of her.

2. The Sack (2:9)

vs. 9. Nineveh had been captured, its palace destroyed, its resistance broken, and its inhabitants thrown into terror-filled flight. Then the scene suddenly shifts from the fleeing populace to the invading conquerors looting the city. The verse has been dramatically translated: "Loot the silver! Loot the gold! There seems to be no end of treasures. Her vast uncounted wealth is stripped away."[4] Nineveh's great treasures, spoils of Assyria's many conquests, became the loot of the victors.

---

[4]Kenneth N. Taylor, *Living Prophecies: The Minor Prophets Paraphrased.* (Wheaton: Tyndale House, 1965), p. 121.

for there is no end of the store. Nineveh was the richest city of its day. Ancient writers confirm that there were great treasuries accumulated in this city, the results of repeated campaigns by the greedy Assyrian empire builders. According to unsubstantiated traditions, some of the city's wealth had been smuggled out during the siege, but most of it fell into the hands of the victors because the Ninevites in their precipitous flight were able to salvage but few possessions of value. The annals of Nabopolassar (Babylonian king) describe the capture of the city by a coalition of Medes and Babylonians as follows: "By the bank of the Tigris they marched against Nineveh: a mighty assault they made upon the city, and in the month Ab . . . a great havoc of the chief men was made. . . . The spoil of the city, a quantity beyond counting, they plundered. and turned the city into a mound and a ruin."[5]

B. THE DESOLATION OF THE CITY (2:10-13)

The desolation of the sacked city is described in a series of seven startled exclamations which summarize its utter devastation as well as the paralysis and helplessness of its remaining inhabitants. In contrast to her former abundance of everything which she could desire, Nineveh is now pictured as completely "cleaned out." No longer is she the "lion" of her day. Divine patience had at last been exhausted; now Jehovah of host was against her.

1. Description (2:10)

vs. 10. *She is empty and void and waste.* The once influential and wealthy city is pictured as desolate, plundered, and destroyed. In three words the prophet depicted how completely Nineveh was overthrown and pillaged. The synonyms, each succeeding one lengthened by the addition of an extra syllable, are difficult to render in English. The words of the original carry the idea of emptiness, while *sack, sacking, ransacking* give something of the similarity of sound in the Hebrew rendering.

the heart melteth, the knees smite together, anguish is in all

---

[5]J. B. Pritchard, *Ancient Near Eastern Texts Relating to the Old Testament* (Princeton: Princeton University Press, 1950), p. 304.

loins, and the faces . . . are waxed pale. Nahum turned from the description of national ruin to individual terror on the part of the once proud populace. The heart of the people was now melted like wax. They could no more form a plan of resistance. Terror and consternation gripped them; their knees trembled and anguish was the lot of their loins. Their faces assumed the ashen color of those completely overcome with fear.

2. Derision (2:11-12)

vss. 11-12. The prophet used the figure of the lion to describe Assyria's power, rapacity, and perhaps the fear of her in which the rest of the world lived. Nineveh had indeed been the den where the Assyrian Lion had stored his booty after his many raids on helpless peoples. And this lion was so powerful that he could make his forays on distant nations without fear that his den would be molested in his absence, for "none made him afraid." But Nahum envisioned the time when this "king of beasts" would be no more. In derision he asked, "Where is the den of the lions . . . ?" The figure of the lion was frequently used in Assyrian reliefs and decorations, and the Assyrian rulers in their boastful self-appraisals often compared themselves to lions. So the prophet mockingly used the same term which in picture and inscription represented Assyrian might and cruelty.

3. Decree (2:13)

vs. 13. Nahum had a religious reason for the disappearance of Nineveh from human history. Jehovah of hosts had decreed it: "Behold, I am against thee." This statement is expressed in Hebrew in two words, a brevity which gives emphasis to the expression. Nineveh's destruction had been decreed by Jehovah of hosts, the Lord of all created things, and he is adequate in power to accomplish his purpose. Both fire and sword had been prominent instruments of destruction in Assyria's conquests. God would now turn them upon her to accomplish his judgment. No more will Nineveh be permitted to "prey" upon weaker nations; no more will the voice of her "messengers" be heard demanding tribute and submission. This will be true simply because "Jehovah of hosts" has decreed her doom.

III. THE VINDICATION OF GOD'S VENGEANCE ON NINEVEH (3:1-7)

For a moment, at least, the prophet's passionate description of the fall of the city (chap. 2) gives way to a more reasoned explanation of the necessity for its destruction.

A. THE VICE OF THE CITY (3:1, 4)

vs. 1. *Woe to the bloody city.* In ancient times the capital of a kingdom or empire was virtually the kingdom; thus there is ascribed to Nineveh all the qualities and characteristics of the Assyrian people. This is more or less true in modern times; for example, that which characterises Washington, D.C. is considered as representative of America as a whole. Nineveh is described as "the bloody city," literally, "a city of bloods." In the original language the plural form denoted *shed blood* or the guilt involved in its shedding (cf. Ps. 51:14; Ezek. 24:6 ff.). "Bloody city" was a fitting epithet for the doomed capital, since the Assyrians were among the most cruel and bloodthirsty peoples known to history. Assyrian monuments graphically and frightfully describe how captives were skinned alive, decapitated, impaled alive, or hanged by hands and feet to die a slow death. Their royal inscriptions boastfully record the number of enemies killed, captives carried off, and cities razed and plundered. But this planned cruelty systematically executed by the "bloody city" was now to be avenged.

it is all full of lies and rapine. Nineveh was not only cruel, it was also a city of deception. It was filled with falsehood and fraud in both business and politics, and especially in relations with other nations. Within the realm as without, truce-breaking and broken promises were all too frequent. Nineveh was also filled with "rapine" or robbery. The word for "rapine" refers to an act of violence and here denotes the violence of the Assyrians in dealing with conquered peoples. Nineveh had despoiled other nations, filling her own coffers with the pillage and plunder of subject peoples.

The prey departeth not. The word for "prey" denotes a tearing or rending, as a wild animal rips or tears its victim. Perhaps the prophet continued the figure of a lion begun in 2:11. Nineveh was indeed like a ferocious lion, continually plundering helpless peoples. In the words "the prey departeth not," the prophet presents a synopsis of Assyria's history, a history marked by endless pillage and rapine.

vs. 4. As Nahum further vindicated God's vengeance upon Nineveh, he compared her conduct to the "whoredoms of a well-favored harlot." Such a figure for sinful nations and cities was a favorite one with the Biblical writers. It was frequently applied to the nation Israel and meant, first of all, infidelity or unfaithfulness to Jehovah, by serving other gods (see Ezek. 23:27; Hos. 4:12). It came also to be applied to political alliances with other nations, for such trust in their might and power betrayed a lack of dependence upon Jehovah (cf. Isa. 33:1-3; Hos. 7:7 ff.). Finally, commercial intercourse of one nation with another was called "whoredom," even when the religious idea was missing (see Isa. 23:17). This is the application of the figure here. As the harlot has her favors for hire, so Nineveh, like a scheming prostitute, has peddled her power to many peoples, always to her own advantage. As a "woman of the street" artfully displays her charms for the purpose of enticing and ruining men, Assyria had beguiled and ensnared nations to their utter destruction. The emphasis then is not upon Assyrian idolatry and its gross immoralities, though to have designated it as "whoredoms" would have been especially fitting; rather, the prophet's point of view is Nineveh's use of intrigue and trickery, of flattery and high-sounding promises in order to satisfy her passion for power, her lust for plunder, and her insatiable appetite for world supremacy. To accomplish these unholy ambitions she "sold nations through her whoredoms and families through her witchcrafts." Cuneiform records provide ample evidence of the fact that the Assyrians did enslave entire nations and that through guile and treacherous dealing they did relegate "families" (smaller nations or racial groups) into slavery.

B. THE RESULT OF THE CITY'S VICE – JUDGMENT (3: 2-3, 5-7)

In Chapter 1 Nahum established the principle that God consistently acts in accordance with his character, and that his government of the universe always coincides with the essential nature of his being. As this principle is applied in relationship to people, it always results in God's intimate concern for his friends (see 1:7) and in his ultimate destruction of his foes (see 1:8). When this principle is applied to the vice-filled city of Nineveh only one result is possible – God's judgment. As the prophet announced "Woe on the bloody city" (3:1) there came again within the range of his vision the final battle signaling her doom (cf. 2:1 ff.).

vs. 2. *The noise of the whip . . . and bounding chariots.* Nahum describes the sounds of the advance of the besieging armies. Again, as in 2:4, 5, he centers his attention on the outstanding weapon of the attack equipment, the chariotry. He hears, as it were, the charioteers' cracking of whips, the rumble of chariot wheels, the galloping horses, and the jolting chariots.

vs. 3. *The horseman mounting [charging], and the flashing sword, and the glittering spear.* The victorious assailants are now in the city, joined in deadly combat with its defenders. The prophet sees the charging horsemen, the flashing swords, the glittering spears, and the dead defenders.

and a multitude of slain . . . they stumble upon their bodies. The multitude of dead and the endless corpses are those of the Ninevites. In this siege there was no time for burying the dead, as important as this act was in the ancient world, and the living stumbled over the heaps of the slain. God's judgment had been delayed (by God), but it came. Not only must Nineveh suffer for her cruelties, lies and rapine (3:1), but she must also pay for the whoredoms committed against other nations (3:4).

vs. 5. *Behold, I am against these, saith Jehovah of hosts.* These words are the literal restatement of 2:13a. Such repetition not only adds to the seriousness of the divine threat but also signifies a certainty as to the fulfilment of its penalty. Nineveh's doom cannot be doubted, since God had twice spoken it. And though her punishment may be inflicted by men, it is "Jehovah of hosts" with whom she has to do.

I will uncover thy skirts . . . and I will show the nations thy nakedness. Since Nineveh had played the role of an international harlot, she would in turn suffer the punishment reserved for a harlot, that of public disgrace. The condemnation described refers to the practice of exposing to public view a woman convicted of unchastity (cf. Ezek. 16:35-39; Hos. 2:3). Nineveh's shameless actions will be matched with the shameful exposure of her nakedness to the nations of the world. Disgrace has been added to indignity, as she who disgraced others is now shamefully exposed in their presence.

vs. 6. *I will cast abominable filth upon thee, and make thee vile, and . . . a gazing-stock.* Though God would, of course, work through human agents the first person pronoun (referring to God) adds force to the figure. It has been suggested that prostitutes in ancient times were publically subjected to the humiliating experience of having filth of every kind thrown at them, and finally set up, perhaps in stocks, as a "gazing-stock," that is, as a sight, spectacle, or example for all to see. Such is to be Nineveh's punishment for her harlotries.

vs. 7. *all . . . that look upon thee shall flee . . . and say, Nineveh is laid waste.* Nineveh is so disgraced, dishonored, and contemptible that those who chance by will gaze for only a moment before fleeing from her loathsome ruins as if from a deadly pestilence. And as they flee in utter amazement that Nineveh has been "laid waste," each one asks, "Who will bemoan her?" This rhetorical question indicates that none will feel sorry for her because the punishment is what she deserved. Then the prophet, as if to magnify the wide-spread hatred of the harlotrous city asked, "Whence shall I seek comforters for thee?" Again there is no answer, for there is no one to show her pity. Her calculated cruelties have alienated everyone who could have comforted her in her agony.

IV. THE VERITY OF GOD'S VENGEANCE ON NINEVEH
(3:8-19)

Having defended or vindicated God's judgment upon Nineveh, Nahum now turns to a theme previously considered, namely, the verity of God's judgment upon Nineveh. In Chapter 1 the prophet was confident of the city's punishment, a confidence based upon the character of God. In the second chapter the reality of her punishment was all the more evident as the prophet envisioned the actual destruction of the wicked city and spoke of it as having already occurred. What could have brought more comfort to his people than to have brought them a final word of assurance concerning the verity or truthfulness of his predictions of Nineveh's destruction!

A. THE LESSON FROM NO-AMON (3:8-13)

Perhaps one of Nahum's countrymen expressed doubt about the possibility of Nineveh's fall and called attention to her impregnable position; or possibly the prophet recalled to his own mind this example of Thebes (No-Amon) whose favorable location made its capture difficult, but whose fall had occurred in the lifetime of many of his hearers. At any rate the prophet, anxious to impress upon his listeners the absolute certainty of Nineveh's downfall, asked them to look at the lesson to be learned from the fate of Thebes. His method involved a rhetorical question that implied a negative answer.

vs. 8. *Art thou better than No-Amon?* No-Amon, city of the god Amon (Amun) was the same as Thebes and was favorably situated on the Nile in southern Egypt. This capital city was long a leading city of the world before its capture in 663 B.C. by the Assyrian king, Ashurbanipal. "Art thou better" does not raise the question of moral superiority or worth; rather the prophet is asking Nineveh if she is better located, stronger, and more able to resist invasion than was Thebes. This is made clear from the remaining portion of the verse.

*that was situate among the rivers . . . whose rampart was the
sea, and her wall was of [from] the sea?* The city of Thebes
was located on both banks of the Nile, whose waters were led
to the gateways of the city's many temples by canals. It was to
these canals and the river that Nahum referred when he spoke of
its being "situate among the rivers, that had the waters round
about her." In Biblical usage the word "sea" often refers to
rivers (cf., e.g., Isa. 27:1; Jer. 51:36). "Rampart" suggests some
type of outer defense before the main defense walls of a city.
For Thebes the outer line of defense (rampart) was the Nile
with its network of moats and canals. Her second line of
defense was the city wall itself which "was from the sea," that is,
it arose at the very edge of the water. Nineveh was no better
situated than No-Amon. Yet this Egyptian city with its seemingly impregnable defenses fell. How, then could Nineveh expect to escape?

vs. 9. *Ethiopia and Egypt were her strength. . . . Put and
Lubim were thy [her] helpers.* No-Amon was much better off
than Nineveh, for while the latter had alienated her neighbors,
the former had formed advantageous alliances. At this particular time Egypt and Ethiopia (Heb. Cush), the country south of
Upper Egypt, were virtually one, inasmuch as the twenty-fifth
or Ethiopian dynasty was on the throne (728-662 B.C.), with
No-Amon or Thebes as its capital. This city as the center of
the Ethiopian empire could depend upon the strength and resources of the entire Nile country, a strength described by
Nahum as "infinite." In addition to Ethiopia and Egypt two
other countries are named as formidable allies of No-Amon.
"Put and Lubim were thy helpers," Nahum declared, apparently
addressing the Ethiopian capital (No-Amon). The location of
Put is still not certain. Although the prophet seems to dis-
tinguish between the two, some identify Put and Lubim as the
same territory, Libya, located generally west of Egypt. Present
consensus, however equates Put with Punt, modern Somaliland
in eastern Africa. The "Lubim" referred to here are the Libyans
of north Africa.

vs. 10. *Yet was she carried away . . . into captivity.* The
words are emphatic, "Yet she, she was carried away," impregnable, populous, prosperous though she was. Thus Nahum came
to the climax of the truth to be derived from his allusion to

Thebes. Despite the advantages of her natural location and the strength of her many allies, she came to an ignoble end, suffering a dismal defeat at the hands of the Assyrian king, Ashurbanipal.

her young also were dashed in pieces at the head of all the streets. This cruel practice on the part of the Assyrians not only relieved them of the added burden and responsibility of transporting children as they carried away much of the captive population, but it also insured the extermination of the whole future population of this people. Such unbelievable barbarity was not infrequent in Bible times (cf. Hos. 10:14; Isa. 13:16; II Kings 8:12). This inhuman act was committed "at the head of all the streets," probably at the crossing of major thoroughfares, where the atrocities would be more sensational and could be viewed by larger groups of spectators. All of this was done in contemptuous disregard of the laws of both man and God.

they cast lots for her honorable men . . . her great men were bound in chains. As a further act of humiliation, the captors treated the nobles as slaves, regarding them merely as so much plunder to be distributed by lot. A final indignity suffered by the captive nobles was that of wearing fetters as they marched into captivity.

vs. 11. It remained only for the prophet to apply the truths taught from the tragic end of Thebes. The basic lesson is simple: if that city fell, in spite of its favorable location and strong allies, how can Nineveh, less favorably located and with no allies, expect to escape destruction?

Thou also shalt be drunken . . . shalt be hid . . . shalt seek a stronghold. The meaning of the first clause is either that Nineveh would be overthrown in the midst of a drunken orgy or that she would have to drink to the full the cup of God's wrath (cf. Isa. 51:17, 21-23; Jer. 25:15-28), and hence become drunk. The latter idea is more likely although the former has some evidence in its favor. According to the historian Diodorus Siculus the Assyrian king and his nobles were surprised (attacked) during one of their drunken carousings, and the city of Nineveh was taken without great effort (cf. 1:10). "Thou shalt be hid," that is, vanish from sight, disappear, become obscure or unknown. When Nineveh fell to the combined thrust of Babylonians, Medes, and Scythians in 612 B.C. the city was reduced to obscurity and covered by its own ruins. In its last days the city doubtless did "seek a stronghold" or defense against its enemies. But it sought in vain, and every stronghold where the Assyrians attempted to make a stand, soon collapsed under the ferocious assault of the invaders.

vss. 12-13. Continuing his emphasis that the fate of Nineveh would parallel that of No-Amon (Thebes), the prophet pointed to the weakness of both her defense and defenders.

All thy fortresses shall be like fig-trees. The point of the prophet's comparison is introduced by the qualifying addition, "with the first-ripe figs" and completed with the description, "If they be shaken, they fall into the mouth of the eater." First-ripe figs can be gathered with a minimum of exertion; a mere shake of the tree and they fall, as it were, into the mouth of the gatherer. Just so, Nineveh's fortress would fall to the enemy with little effort on his part.

Behold, thy people in the midst of thee are women. With the outer defenses overcome the defenders within the city itself become demoralized and panic-stricken. Thus they are unable to acquit themselves as men and offer no more opposition to the enemy than terrified, defenseless women.

the gates of the land are . . . open unto thine enemies; the fire hath devoured thy bars. The natural entrances to the city with their fortifications have been taken by the invader; hence, it is as if the gates themselves were opened, for the enemy can now approach the city walls. "Bars," made either of metal or of wood, were commonly used to close and strengthen the gates of cities (see Deut. 3:5; Neh. 3:3). Here, however, and parallel in usage to "gates of the land," bars refer to the fortresses and barriers located outside Nineveh's walls. The enemy would destroy these by fire.

B. A DIRGE OF DOOM (3:14-19)

Nahum turns again to the final attack against Nineveh and pours out his derisive invectives upon the doomed city. He uses the same verb forms (infinitive absolute) as previously (cf. 2:1) in giving his terse instruction to Nineveh to prepare for her inevitable fate.

vs. 14. *Draw thee water . . . strengthen thy fortress; go into the clay.* These exhortations were all given in irony. In essence the prophet was saying, "Prolong your resistance. It will not benefit you for your fall is certain" (cf. vs. 15). Nevertheless, he urged them to see to the water supply, an important item in case of a long siege. Apparently much of Nineveh's drinkable water supply came from outside the city proper, and could be cut off with little difficulty by an invader. In addition to securing a water supply Nineveh must defend herself; therefore the prophet called upon her to "strengthen thy fortress" or to make strong all her defenses. To do this bricks were needed; therefore, the people were admonished, "Go into the clay, tread the mortar, lay hold of the brick mold."

vs. 15. *There shall the fire devour thee; the sword shall cut thee off.* "There" is emphatic. There, right there at the very spot where the Ninevites were strengthening the fortress or making the bricks for their strengthening, the fire would consume them and the sword would bring them low. Ancient history and modern archaeological finds give witness to the fact that the primary agent in Nineveh's destruction was fire.

it will devour thee like the cankerworm. That is, like the cankerworm (better, locust) *devours.* "It" probably refers to both fire and sword, that is, the devastation by fire and sword would be as swift and complete as that wrought on vegetation by these greedy insects.

make thyself many as the cankerworm . . . as the locust. The prophet having begun the picture of locusts as he compared the destructive power of Nineveh's enemies to that of this common Palestinian insect, continues the figure as he suddenly turned and compared the people of Nineveh to locusts. The statement is conditional, "Though you make yourself many as the locust," that is, although you multiply yourself as rapidly as the locust or cankerworm (this last term probably indicates one of the stages in the life cycle of the locust), you cannot escape. A striking characteristic of locusts is their amazing power of reproduction. But deliverance for Nineveh is not to be found in numbers. Even if her defenders were as numerous as a horde of locusts, she still could not escape God's judgment.

vs. 16. *Thou has multiplied thy merchants above the stars of heaven.* Because of her location Nineveh was able to engage in extensive and profitable commerce with other countries. Numerous major trade routes led to this city and radiated from it into all parts of the world. It was the commerical center of the ancient world, where countless merchants, "multiplied above the stars," and trade representatives from other countries did a flourishing business.

the cankerworm ravageth, and fleeth away. The meaning is difficult. As related to the "merchants" (above) the interpretation seems to be, that as the locust (cankerworm) brings sudden devastation and then just as suddenly is gone, in the instantaneous and certain destruction of Nineveh there will be a like disappearance of the merchants. These "plunderers," numbering more than the "stars of heaven" will suddenly disappear, and their plunder with them.

vs. 17. *Thy princes are as the locusts, and thy marshals as swarms of grasshoppers.* Nahum has shown that military power will not save Nineveh (vs. 15), and that she cannot be delivered by her riches accumulated through commerce (vs. 16); now he seeks to set out the fact that her officials cannot be her salvation. These officials are likened to "locusts" and "grasshoppers" with wings made stiff and lifeless by the evening cold, which, after being warmed by the rays of the sun regain their strength and disappear. Two points of comparison are pertinent. These Assyrian leaders are like locusts in cold weather, inept and inert, powerless to do anything in their city's crisis. And as the locust, when warmed rises and flies away, so will these leaders flee in the face of danger, never to be seen again.

vs. 18. *Thy shepherds slumber, O king of Assyria; thy nobles are at rest.* The Assyrian king is addressed in grim words as he is informed of the death of his "shepherds" (used of rulers and leaders) and "nobles." They are at rest in the sleep of death.

thy people are scattered upon the mountains . . . none to gather them. With their leaders gone the people of Nineveh can no longer offer effective resistance to their enemies. They are therefore "scattered upon the mountains" where they have fled for safety. "There is none to gather them," Nineveh is wiped out forever.

vs. 19. *There is no assuaging of thy hurt; thy wound is grievous.* Since Nineveh will be no more and the Assyrian kingship is inescapably doomed, it is fitting that the dirge should end with words of warning addressed to the capital, "There is no healing of thy hurt, thy injury is serious." The damage sustained by the fall of Nineveh and the subsequent dissolution of the empire can never be repaired. Both city and empire vanished from history.

all that hear the report of thee clap their hands. As Nahum could find no one to comfort Nineveh (3:7), so also he found that all who heard of her utter destruction rejoiced at her fate. The surrounding nations "clap their hands" with joy at the news of Nineveh's end, for it will also mean the end of her cruel and ceaseless oppression.

for upon whom hath not thy wickedness passed continually? Joy over Nineveh's fall was universal for her wickedness was universal. Nahum thus ends his "dirge of doom" on a theological note (see 1:2 ff.). Nineveh's end was the result of her sin, sin against God and her fellow man. A righteous God, in patience and mercy may delay punishment, but he never remits punishment without repentance on the part of the sinner. Nineveh refused to repent; hence, her doom was inevitable.

BIBLIOGRAPHY

Davidson, A. B., *Nahum, Habakkuk and Zephaniah,* "The Cambridge Bible Series." Cambridge: The University Press, 1896.

Dunning, H. Ray, "Beacon Bible Commentary," Vol. V. Kansas City: Beacon Hill Press, 1966.

Eiselen, F. C., *Prophecy and the Prophets.* New York: Eaton & Mains, 1913.

Farrar, F. W., *The Minor Prophets.* London: James Nisbet and Co. (n.d.).

Feinberg, Charles L., *Nahum,* "The Wycliffe Bible Commentary." Nashville: Abingdon Press, 1929.

Gailey, James H., *The Book of Nahum,* "The Layman's Bible Commentary." Richmond: John Knox Press, 1962.

Graham, William C., *Nahum,* "The Abingdon Bible Commentary." Nashville: Abingdon Press, 1929.

Maier, W. A., *The Book of Nahum.* St. Louis: Concordia Publishing House, 1959.

Smith, G. A., *The Book of the Twelve Prophets,* Vol. II. New York: Harper and Brothers, 1928.

Taylor, Charles L., *Nahum* (Exegesis), "The Interpreter's Bible," Vol. VI. New York: Abingdon Press, 1956.

THE BOOK OF ZEPHANIAH

INTRODUCTION

Zephaniah and Nahum belonged to the same age and in all probability prophesied within a few years of each other. Which of the two came first is still a debated question. It is the view of the writer that Zephaniah was the first to break a prophetic silence of some three-quarters of a century since Isaiah's day as he publicly raised his voice against the apostasy and degeneracy of Judah. The two prophets present a pronounced contrast. While Nahum announced the particular judgment of Nineveh alone, and saw in that judgment the hope of Judah's liberation from Assyrian tyranny, Zephaniah proclaimed the rapid approach of a universal judgment whose first and chief severity must fall upon Jerusalem. Nahum regarded the judgment of Nineveh as just retribution for her crimes. Zephaniah looked upon God's judgment of Judah and the nations not simply as punishment due them, but as the means by which the cleansing of Judah and the conversion of the nations would be accomplished. Thus, in breadth of view and clarity of insight into the ultimate course of divine design or purpose, Zephaniah is far superior to Nahum.

Knowledge concerning Zephaniah, which is scanty, is confined entirely to the information given in the book bearing his name. While there are three other men in the Old Testament with the same name (see I Chron. 6:36; Jer. 21:1; Zech. 6:10), there is no valid reason for connecting any of them with the prophet. The name "Zephaniah" (Greek and Latin Bibles "Sophonias") means "Jehovah hides," or "he whom Jehovah hath hidden." The prophet was doubtless born during the ruthless reign of King Manasseh (687-641 B.C.), who "shed innocent blood very much, till he had filled Jerusalem from one end to another" (II Kings 21:16). Zephaniah's name, therefore, indicated a confidence in the power of God to hide (protect) his worshiper or follower in times of danger. George L. Robinson has further suggested that the name has "a significance which especially fits the prophet's message. His personality, in fact, is imbedded in his message."[1]

As is true of others of the prophets (e.g., Isaiah, Jeremiah, Joel, and Zechariah), Zephaniah's ancestry is given (see 1:1). It is, however, unique with this prophet that his genealogy is traced back through four generations to one named "Hizkiah." The identity of this individual is problematical. Presumably, he is to be identified with Hezekiah, an outstanding king of Judah (716-687 B.C.), otherwise what would be the reason for listing his ancestry as far back as the fourth generation. That he was a member of the royal family is supported by the rather intimate knowledge he shows of the court and the princes of Judah (see 1:8; 3:3), as well as the evidence which indicates that he was a citizen of Jerusalem (see 1:4, 10, 11). It has also been suggested that the long genealogy may have resulted from a Hebrew girl's marrying a foreigner. Since the offspring of such a union would not be accepted or admitted to the Jewish community unless he could show a pure Jewish pedigree for at least three generations (cf. Deut. 23:8), in the case of Zephaniah (whose father was a foreigner?) such a genealogy was shown.[2]

According to the title verse (see 1:1),[3] Zephaniah's ministry occurred "in the days of Josiah the son of Amon, king of Judah," that is, somewhere between 639-608 B.C. But is it possible to more definitely locate the prophet's ministry within the thirty-one years of Josiah's rule? This king's reign falls rather naturally into two periods, separated by the great reform movement which began in 621 B.C. with the finding of the Book of the Law in the Temple (see II Kings 22). Numerous scholars date Zephaniah's ministry in the first period, that is, prior to 621 B.C. Arguments adduced in favor of this view are: (1) the extreme youth of King Josiah, who came to the throne of Judah at the age of eight years, would have made it rather easy for the royal princes to have practiced the excesses condemned in 1:8-9; (2) the idola-

---

[1] *The Twelve Minor Prophets* (Grand Rapids: Baker Book House, 1952), p. 130.

[2] Emil Kraeling, *Commentary on the Prophets, Vol. II* (Camden: Thomas Nelson & Sons, 1966), p. 260.

[3] For a discussion of the reliability of evidence found in the title verse, see the author's *The Book of Micah*, "Shield Bible Study Outlines" (Grand Rapids: Baker Book House, 1968), pp. 17 f.

trous practices so severely condemned by Zephaniah in 1:3-5 are the very ones abolished in the reformation under Josiah; (3) the mood or temper of the times as indicated by Zephaniah's words in 1:12 is better understood if these words were uttered prior to 621 B.C. With the beginning of the reform movement by Josiah during that year, religious enthusiasm seems to have continued until his death in 608 B.C.; (4)it seems evident that at the time of the delivery of this prophecy an enemy was seriously threatening Judah and the surrounding nations. Surely the most dreaded foe during the last quarter of the seventh century B.C. was the Scythians, wild, fierce tribes from the territory now occupied by Russia, who swept in great hordes over Western Asia and Syria and were poised to invade Egypt, when Pharaoh Psammitichus I bought them off with rich gifts.

Evidently, Zephaniah sensed in the presence of these cruel barbarians and fearless robbers God's terrible scourge of the nations, including Judah, for their wickedness. To the prophet the Scythians were the executioners of the Divine judgment upon his sinful countrymen and upon the surrounding nations. In them he saw the harbingers of the "day of Jehovah" (see 1:7, 14). From the occasion of their coming Zephaniah's prophecies may be fairly accurately dated as between 630 and 625 B.C., the period of the Scythian invasion of the nations of Western Asia. Thus, since the reforms of King Josiah did not really begin until 621 B.C. with the finding of the Book of the Law by Hilkiah the priest, it seems safe to conclude that the ministry of Zephaniah preceded rather than followed, the religious reformation under Josiah.[4] In fact, many scholars are of the opinion that the prophecies of Zephaniah helped to prepare the way for Josiah and those who sought to aid him in the reform movement.[5] If these conclusions regarding the date of Zephaniah's ministry are valid, it is evident that he was contemporary with the

---

[4]For discussion of a later date for his ministry, see J. P. Hyatt, *Journal of Near Eastern Studies*, VII (1948), 25-29. For a contrary view relative to the place of the Scythians in Zephaniah's prophecies, see H. L. Ellison, *Men Spake from God* (London: The Paternoster Press, 1958), pp. 68, 81.

[5]See, e.g., B. W. Anderson, *Understanding the Old Testament* (Englewood Cliffs: Prentice-Hall, Inc., 1957), pp. 289 ff.; J. T. Carson, "Zephaniah," *The New Bible Commentary"* (London: Inter-Varsity Fellowship, 1953), pp. 736 f.

prophet Jeremiah, at least during the early years of his (Jeremiah's) ministry (cf. Jer. 1:1 f.).

The prophets, like all other men, were influenced by the period in which they lived. Zephaniah was no exception. The harsh note of his message is scarcely understandable apart from a knowledge of the tenor of his times. For a complete picture of the day in which Zephaniah lived, it is necessary to look backward to the death of King Hezekiah (687 B.C.) shortly after the close of the eighth century. With the death of this good king the golden age of Hebrew prophecy came to an end. Outstanding prophetic personalities were yet to come, but never again was the call of God heard and heeded by men of the high caliber of Amos, Hosea, Isaiah, and Micah. "In the brief fifty years which brought the eighth century to its glorious close they had lifted the religion of Israel out of the semi-darkness which had swathed it for a thousand years, and floodlit the Hill of Zion with a light that has ever since guided and inspired the world."[6]

At the beginning of the seventh century, however, this light seemed to have been completely and hopelessly extinguished. Manasseh, Hezekiah's son and successor, was hardly seated on his royal throne before it was obvious that he was one of the worst characters that had ever held the scepter of David, and the period of his reign has been fittingly characterized as "the dark ages of the history of Judah." It seemed that he determined to undo everything that his father Hezekiah, strongly encouraged by Isaiah, had accomplished. To preach the God of Isaiah became a crime. "Back to the old!" was the popular cry to which Manasseh and the princes of his court listened. The "high places," pulled down by Hezekiah (see II Kings 21:3), were defiantly rebuilt by his son; altars were again set up to Ashtoreth (Canaanite goddess), Chemosh (Moabite god), Milcom (Ammonite god), and to local Baals (gods) all over Judah. The abomination of heathen altars was found even within the Temple itself, and the hosts of the heavens were worshiped just as in Nineveh. Manasseh thus strengthened his position not only with his subjects, many of whom were antagonistic to the

---

[6]Stephen L. Caiger, *Lives of the Prophets* (New York: Macmillan Company, 1958), p. 156.

worship of Jehovah, but with his Assyrian masters as well. Furthermore the degrading superstitions of witchcraft and augury were again practiced in the land, and immorality under the pretext of religion was a common occurrence. The apex of his idolatrous practices was reached with the renewal of the abominable rite of child sacrifice (see II Kings 21). According to II Chron. 33:11-19, Manasseh experienced a change of heart after he had been arrested on orders from the Assyrian monarch. However, the depth and permanency of the change are highly questionable (cf. II Chron. 33:22). At any rate all that Hezekiah had accomplished seems to have been undone by his son.

In view of these actions on the part of the Hebrew monarch, it is not difficult to understand why Manasseh has been called "the arch idolater of Hebrew history." In fact idols came to have such an integral part in his life and experience that he even named a son after an Egyptian deity, Amon. This son later succeeded his father on the throne of Judah but reigned too brief a time (two years) to accomplish anything in the way of religious reform even if he had desired to do so, and the Biblical writer informs us that he had no such intentions (see II Kings 21:20 ff.). His assassination left his eight-year-old son, Josiah, in nominal control of the affairs of state. Because of Josiah's youth the status of the kingdom, religious-wise at least, remained for some time very much as they had been during the reigns of his father and grandfather. As a matter of fact it was some eighteen years before the initiation of a reform movement (see II Kings 22:3 ff.).

If our assumption is correct that Zephaniah prophesied early in the reign of Josiah, that is, prior to 621 B.C., his prophecies give witness to the fact that religious conditions in the early years of Josiah's reign were very similar to those during the reign of his grandfather Manasseh (cf., e.g., Zeph. 1:4-6). Idolatrous rites which Manasseh had introduced (re-introduced) flourished unchecked; idolatrous priests were maintained at public expense; the worship of strange deities was openly tolerated; and the adoration of sun, moon, and stars was extensively practiced. Many had openly forsaken the true faith, and a still larger number were atheists at heart, carelessly mouthing, "Jehovah will not do good, neither will he do evil" (1:12). With this practical apostasy from Jehovah there was combined a spirit of moral lawlessness. The very bonds of society were loosened. The sins of the ruling classes especially (see 1:8 f.) had made Jerusalem ripe for judgment.

To announce this judgment God had his spokesman standing behind the curtain waiting for the cue to come to the front and center of the stage. This spokesman (Zephaniah) did not have long to wait. Ominous events were transpiring outside of Judah. The power of Assyria was beginning to crumble even during its greatest expansion under Ashurbanipal (668-626 B.C.). During his last appearances in Palestine (*ca.* 665 and 647 B.C.), he did not even attempt to reconquer Egypt, which had earlier revolted. It was becoming increasingly clear that Assyrian power was on the wane and that the nations of Media and Babylon were forging to the front in terms of world leadership. In addition a third power had made its appearance on the political horizon and posed serious threats not only to Assyria but to the other nations of the world including Judah. As early as 650 B.C. savage tribes of Scythians swept across from what is now southern Russia, spread over the entire area between the Black and the Caspian Seas, and according to Herodotus, the Greek historian, advanced southward as far as Syria and even to Egypt.[7] They were a cruel and ferocious people and have been described as fighting "with bow and arrow from the saddle and drinking the blood of their enemies from vessels made from their skulls."[8] Although Judah was never invaded the exploits of these savage tribesmen filled all men with fear and thoughts of terrible disaster. Zephaniah shared with others a sense of impending doom and saw in this "scourge of the nations" what others did not see — the judgment of God. Hence the prophet looked upon the Scythians as the instrument of God's judgment upon his own sinful nation and he sensed in the movements of these ravaging hordes the foreboding of the great "day of Jehovah." Keenly conscious of the righteousness of God and the sins of his own people, Zephaniah envisioned the approaching day of doom and announced its coming in words that "pierced the complacent atmosphere of Jerusalem like a trumpet."

---

[7]Charles L. Taylor, *Zephaniah*, "Interpreter's Bible," Vol. VI (Nashville: Abingdon Press, 1956), p. 1008.

[8]Ernest G. Braham, *The Prophets of Israel* (London: George Gill & Sons, 1948), p. 62.

Numerous scholars hold that the Book of Zephaniah has been revised by editors and thus deny authorship of a major portion of its contents to the prophet named in the opening verse of Chapter 1 (see 1:1). A study of these views reveals that there is much disagreement as to the reasons for denying authorship to Zephaniah and still greater differences of opinion as to the verses that are assigned to an editor(s). In regard to the latter, the authenticity of every verse in Chapters 2 and 3 and several verses in Chapter 1 has been questioned by one or more scholars. The reasons for the denial of these passages (individually or collectively) to Zephaniah are in general two in number: (1) a phraseology or circle of ideas appears in them which is characteristic of a period later than Zephaniah's day, to which period they must be assigned; and (2) difference in tone when compared to passages attributed to Zephaniah. It must be admitted that there are certain terms in the Book of Zephaniah which are extensively used in exilic and post-exilic times (e.g., "meek of the earth," and "seek meekness" in 2:3), but it has never been shown conclusively that these words could not have been used as early as Zephaniah's time. In regard to a difference in tone, is it logical to conclude, for example, that 2:1-3 is by a different hand from that which wrote 1:2-18 solely on the basis of a difference in spirit in the two passages? Could not the same prophet who spoke the harsh and condemnatory words of judgment in Chapter 1 also have uttered the words of comfort and hope found in the opening verses (1-3) of Chapter 2? The prophets usually were not content with bare threats and announcements of judgment. With God's spokesmen judgment was not the final word; in their thought it always served a disciplinary purpose. The prophets always seemed to offer hope — at least to a remnant. Presently, therefore, there seem to be no sufficient reasons for denying to Zephaniah any portion of the prophecy bearing his name.[9]

Zephaniah has been described as a man with one idea that overwhelmed and overpowered him, the idea of judgment. This

---

[9]For a fuller discussion of authorship, see A. B. Davidson, *"Nahum, Habakkuk, and Zephaniah,* "The Cambridge Bible Commentary" (Cambridge: The University Press, 1896), pp. 99-107; Also, see Charles L. Taylor, *Ibid.,* pp. 1009 ff.

overpowering sense of judgment found expression in the prophet's use of the term "day of Jehovah." While certainly not the first prophet to make use of this expression, Zephaniah developed the idea with vigor and depth of detail. At least a century earlier Amos had sought to correct the popular concept of the day (see 5:18-20) in the mind of his people. For them the day of the Lord would be a day when the people of God would triumph over their enemies, a day when the Lord would bring complete destruction upon the Gentile nations of the world. They, therefore, desired and cried out for the day's coming. Amos sought to transform this concept into a day of ethical import when God would manifest himself against sin wherever he found it, whether among his own people or the foreigner. "Amos thus transformed a popular idea; and the prophets used the expression in this transformed sense to denote the day on which Jehovah is conceived as manifesting Himself in His fullness, striking down wrong and illusion and human pride, and giving the final victory to righteousness and truth."[10]

Zephaniah was doubtless influenced by both Amos and Isaiah (cf. Isa. 2:12 ff.). Also, due to the fact that the prophet was probably living under the threat of invasion by the barbaric Scythians, he conceived of the "day of Jehovah" under the imagery of invasion and war. In these restless hordes from the north, the prophet saw the approach of the day of doom. In anticipation of its gloom and terror, he depicted in vivid language the supernatural agencies taking part with the war of men in a visitation by God. With stern words he declared the purposes of the Lord in wreaking his wrath upon the earth. In the shock of earthquake, the tumult of war, and the hot fires of judgment, God would make known his holiness and his sovereignty over all other gods as well as nations.

Zephaniah, however, felt free to modify the concept of the day of Jehovah. For earlier prophets the day was a crisis in the world which was a definite point in history. The events surrounding its coming though tumultuous were natural, and when the day had passed history would again resume its ceaseless flow. But Zephaniah conceived of the day as a terminal event

---

[10]S. R. Driver, *The Minor Prophets,* "The Century Bible," ed. Walter F. Adney (New York: Oxford University Press, 1906), p. 115.

with manifestations of the supernatural. In grim colors he wove the tapestry of God's judgment from the warp of war and siege and the woof of vague and solemn terrors from another world. History seemed to be swallowed up; the prophet scarcely saw Israel beyond the day. The words of G. A. Smith are appropriate: "In short, with Zephaniah the Day of the Lord tends to become the Last Day. His book is the tinging of prophecy with apocalypse: that is the moment which it supplies in the history of Israel's religion."[11]

While it may be true that Zephaniah adds little to the teachings of previous prophets, it is false to conclude that the book bearing his name is without religious value. Its merit is first found in the moral earnestness and spiritual fervor with which the prophet proclaimed the sublime truth that deliverance from sin (salvation) results only from the work of God. In this emphasis he provided an ever-needed corrective to the idea of salvation by the process of social reform. Of equal value is Zephaniah's emphasis upon the seriousness and certainty of God's judgment. In regard to the reality of this judgment the prophet leaves no room for doubt. Neither men nor nations can flaunt God endlessly. If they do not forsake sin and return to God they will be punished. The sternness of the prophet at this point is nowhere modified in the New Testament. Christ himself spoke of the terror of eternal damnation, and warned that it is better to give up that part of the body which yields to temptation than for the whole body to be cast into hell (see Mark 9: 43 ff.).

---

[11]*The Book of the Twelve Prophets,* Vol. II (New York: Harper and Brothers, 1928), p. 48.

OUTLINE OF THE BOOK OF ZEPHANIAH

I. THE UNIVERSAL JUDGMENT OF GOD (1:1–3:8)
Title Verse (1:1)
   A. Introduction: The Judgment Announced (1:2-3)
   B. Judgment on Jerusalem (1:4–2:3)
      1. The Judgment Defended (1:4-6, 8-9, 12-13)
         a. Baal Worship (1:4c)
         b. Idolatrous Priests (1:4d)
         c. Nature Worship (1:5a)
         d. Syncretistic Worship (1:5b)
         e. Apostasy (1:6a)
         f. Indifference (1:6b, 12-13)
         g. Aping Foreign Fashions (1:8)
         h. Violence and Defeat (1:9)
      2. The Judgment Portrayed (1:7, 14)
      3. The Judgment Described (1:15-18, 10-11)
      4. An Exhortation to Repentance (2:1-3)
   C. Judgment on the Nations (2:4-15)
      1. Judgment on Philistia (2:4-7)
      2. Judgment on Moab and Ammon (2:8-11)
      3. Judgment on Ethiopia (2:12)
      4. Judgment on Assyria (2:13-15)
   D. Judgment Reaffirmed (3:1-8)
      1. On Jerusalem (3:1-7)
      2. On the Nations (3:8)

II. THE UNLIMITED REDEMPTION (DELIVERANCE) OF GOD (3:9-20)
   A. The Promise of Redemption (Conversion) (3:9-13)
      1. To the Heathen (3:9-10)
      2. To the Remnant of Judah (3:11-13)
   B. A Picture of the Redeemed (3:14-20)

I. THE UNIVERSAL JUDGMENT OF GOD
(1:1—3:8)

Title Verse (1:1)

This introductory formula is very similar to that found in a number of the prophetical writings (cf. Hos. 1:1; Joel 1:1; Micah 1:1). It is most unusual, however, that the prophet's ancestry is traced back to the fourth generation. In all probability this was done in order to include some illustrious ancestor; in this case Hezekiah, an outstanding king of Judah (see II Kings 18). If such a conclusion is valid, Zephaniah was of royal descent. This adds interest to his severe condemnation of the royal house for their aping of foreign manners (see 1:8). It also suggests that Zephaniah was a very young man for four generations separate him and his noteworthy ancestor (Hezekiah), spanning a period of approximately one hundred years.

Zephaniah's claim to authority, however, was not derived from his royal lineage; rather, it stemmed from the fact that he spoke *the word of Jehovah.* While his natural descent may have served him well in gaining access to the courts of royalty, it was the supernatural source of his message that gave the prophet a sense of urgency, certainty, and power as he delivered his message. The message was not Zephaniah's; it was from the Lord, the sole source of every truly prophetic word.

Josiah came to the throne of Judah at the age of eight years. His reign lasted for some thirty-one years (639-608 B.C.), ending with his death as his forces fought the Egyptians at Megiddo (II Kings 23:29). The specific time of Zephaniah's ministry in Josiah's reign is difficult to determine, but it seems most likely to have occurred, at least its beginning, prior to 621 B.C. On the problem of the date of the prophet's ministry see the Introduction, pp. 59 ff.

A. THE JUDGMENT ANNOUNCED (1:2-3)

vs. 2. With startling suddenness the prophet began his procla-

69

mation of the universal judgment of God. This divine visitation effected by human instrumentality was to be worldwide in its scope. It would come not only upon *man and beast* but upon *the birds of the heavens and the fishes of the sea.* All creation had corrupted itself before its Maker, similar to the days of Noah, and God had determined to administer justice. In sweeping terms Zephaniah saw God bringing about the destruction of all life from the face of the earth because of the sin of mankind. The prophet seemingly was unaware of the mercy of God, at least initially in his messages. This prompted George Adam Smith to write: "There is no great hope in his book, hardly any tenderness and never a glimpse of beauty . . . he is pitilessly true to his great keynotes: *I will sweep, sweep everything from the face of the ground; he will burn,* burn up everything. No hotter book lies in the Old Testament."[1]

vs. 3. *The stumblingblocks with the wicked.* In the consuming fire of God's judgment not only will the wicked themselves be swept away, but the very objects which have caused them to stumble morally and spiritually will be "utterly consumed." The very things which had been the occasion for transgression will be swept away with the transgressors. "Stumblingblocks" is frequently used with reference to idols (see Ezek. 14:3, 4, 7) and in the light of subsequent verses (esp. 4 and 5) can have that meaning here, although a wider application is possible.

saith Jehovah. The announcement of certain judgment was more than a practical guess of a political seer. It was the oracle (*word, message*) of Jehovah, the sovereign Ruler of the universe. Let all men beware!

B. JUDGMENT ON JERUSALEM (1:4–2:3)

Zephaniah now narrows his vision to encompass only his own people (Judah). They too are guilty of transgression against Jehovah and consequently must experience the refining fire of his judgment. Since Jerusalem was the center of the nation, both politically and religiously, the prophet saw judgment focused upon this capital city. It is interesting to note that Zephaniah, in his specific references to God's judgment, begins with

---

[1]*Op. cit.*, p. 47.

Judah. This is in contrast with the actions of the prophet Amos, who began with other nations and concluded with his own (cf. Amos 1:3–2:6).

1. The Judgment Defended (1:4-6, 8-9, 12-13)

The Lord threatened to *stretch out my hand upon Judah, and upon all the inhabitants of Jerusalem.* This threat resulted from a number of factors.

a. *Baal Worship* (1:4c)

I will cut off the remnant of Baal from this place. "From this place" refers to Jerusalem. This would imply that Zephaniah was a native of that city. "Baal [= lord] was the name of one of the most common ancient deities. When the Israelites entered Canaan they encountered a people who zealously worshipped these gods (*baalim*). Since the natives were largely agriculturists many of their *baalim* were fertility gods whose festivals were connected with immoral practices, "sacred" prostitution, and sexual orgies. God's people were constantly tempted to worship these deities instead of, or in addition to, Jehovah. While Baalism refers primarily to the worship of the god Baal, it came also to be used as a synonym of idolatry in various forms, such as the worship of images of Jehovah or his worship under any false conception of his being. Thus any worship of Jehovah unworthy of his nature or implying an inadequate conception of such, was stigmatized as Baal-worship. Hence, "the remnant of Baal" may refer not only to that which was left of outright Baal-worship but to any inadequate or false worship of Jehovah as well. All that falls short of a genuine, sincere worship of Jehovah will be cut off in the day of his judgment.

Some see in the term "remnant of Baal" the indication of a time following Josiah's attempt to eradicate idolatry — an effort begun in 621 B.C. with the finding of the Book of the Law in the Temple. Consequently Zephaniah's ministry must be dated after the initiation of the reform movement (621 B.C.). Somewhat destructive to this argument is the fact that the Septuagint gives the rendering *names of Baal* for "remnant of Baal" (cf. Hos. 2:17).

b. *Idolatrous Priests* (1:4d)

and the name of the Chemarim with the priest. "Chemarim"

is the usual Aramaic word for priest. It comes from a root whose meaning is *to be black*. Whether the priests were so named because of long black robes which they wore is not known. The word is used in the Old Testament only of idolatrous priests (cf. Hos. 10:5; II Kings 23:5). These along with the degenerate regular priests of Jehovah, those who were false to the true service of God, would be cut off in judgment.

c. *Nature Worship* (1:5a)

And them that worship the host of heaven upon the housetops. Reference is made to the worship of certain Assyrian astral deities which had been introduced into Judah during the evil reign of Manassah (see II Kings 21:3). This worship of the sun, moon, and stars from the roofs of various buildings continued until the time of Zedekiah, the last king of Judah (see Jer. 32:29), in spite of stern warnings against such practices (see Deut. 4:19); 17:3). The flat rooftops of houses in the East were well adapted to the worship of heavenly bodies, since their rising and setting could be better observed from an elevated position.

d. *Syncretistic Worship* (*worship of Jehovah and another god(s)* (1:5b)

and them that worship and that swear by the Lord, and that swear by Malcam. "Malcam" literally means *their king*. According to the Septuagint (and other ancient versions) the correct reading is "Milcom." Some scholars hold that it refers to Molech, the Phoenician god to whom human sacrifices were made (see II Kings 23:10) and whose worship was common in Zephaniah's day. The people then, while rendering lip service to Jehovah, paid homage to Molech as their king. By word of mouth they professed loyalty to God; but in actual practice they swore by a heathen deity and worshiped it. To swear by a deity was to openly acknowledge him, to publicly pledge oneself to his service. Such actions resulted in a divided loyalty, denounced not alone by the prophets but by Christ as well (see Matt. 6:24). Jehovah will be Lord of all or he will not be Lord at all.

e. *Apostasy* (1:6a)

And them that are turned back from following Jehovah. God's judgment is decreed for those who had once followed him but now have "turned back" and have become apostates. Caught up in the mesh of apostasy, they soon became captive to the sensuous, immoral fertility cults of Canaan, and deliberately abandoned the worship of Jehovah.

f. *Indifference* (1:6b, 12-13)

vs. 6b. *and those that have not sought Jehovah nor enquired of him.* These words are descriptive of the inhabitants of Judah who were indifferent to and unconcerned about the things of God. They were perfectly satisfied to live their lives without giving God — his will and his word — any consideration. To enquire of Jehovah is equivalent "to worship in his temple" and finds a parallel in Psalm 10:4, which paraphrased reads, "The wicked in the pride of his countenance does not go to church."[2]

vs. 12. *and I will punish the men that are settled on their lees, that say in their heart, Jehovah will not do good, neither will he do evil.* The ultimate result of indifference to spiritual values is moral stagnation. To describe such a condition the prophet used a striking metaphor from wine-making, "settled on their lees." Perhaps a better translation of "settled" is *thickened, congealed, hardened.* The fermented wine was left for a while on the "lees" (the solid matter which had settled to the bottom) to give it strength and flavor. If left too long the wine became syrupy, too sweet, and unpalatable. In explaining Zephaniah's application of this figure to Judah, Theodore Laetsch has written: "Judah had settled down on its dregs and impurities, until the lusts of its wicked flesh had completely permeated the good wine of sanctification and obedience to the Lord and had changed God's chosen people to a nation hardened in iniquity, equaling and surpassing the Gentiles in moral impurities, shameless vices, and self-satisfied lip-service."[3] Such men quickly settle into an unfeeling indifference or callous incredulity toward the participation of any higher power in the affairs of men. *They say in their heart, Jehovah will not do good, neither will he do evil.* What a revelation the coming judgment will be to these who think that God is morally indifferent!

---

[2]Charles L. Taylor, *op. cit.*, p. 1015.
[3]Theodore Laetsch, *The Minor Prophets*, "Bible Commentary" (Saint Louis: Concordia Publishing House, 1956), p. 361.

In the words, *I will search Jerusalem with lamps,* Zephaniah pictured God searching the city of Jerusalem in order to bring to judgment those who were responsible for the spiritual indifference of the times. Perhaps a large part of the sin of the indifferent is that they hope to escape responsibility by escaping notice. Every age has its masses who have remained obscure, not because of humility but because they were cowardly, lazy or indifferent. However, in the day of God's judgment none of these shall escape. Diligent search will be made for all, either by God or by his agents (the invader). In this verse (12) one sees the "criminal apathy of the well-to-do classes sunk in ease and religious indifference," which called forth from G. A. Smith the classic statement: "The great causes of God and humanity are not defeated by the hot assaults of the devil, but by the slow, crushing, glacier-like mass of thousands and thousands of indifferent nobodies. God's causes are never destroyed by being blown up, but by being sat upon.[4]

vs. 13. For those who lived as if Jehovah were not at work in the world and who denied his providence (vs. 12), the time would come when they would discover from bitter experience how erroneous was their belief. Soon all their possessions would be lost as the result of God's judgment upon them.

And their wealth shall become a spoil, and their houses a desolation. That for which the "indifferent" have lived — their wealth — will become the prey of the enemy. Their houses also will be made empty (desolate) because of the death or captivity of their occupants.

they shall build houses . . . not inhabit them . . . plant vineyards . . . not drink the wine thereof. Both clauses are common expressions signifying that the ones referred to would not enjoy the fruit of their labor (cf. Deut. 28:30; Amos 5:11; Micah 6:15). Judah, because of the judgment of God upon her would not be able to insure to her citizens that to which every man aspires, a home and the fruit of his labors.

g. *Aping Foreign Fashions* (1:8)

I will punish . . . all such as are clothed with foreign apparel. To a degree at least the Lord had regulated the dress of his peo-

---

[4]*Op. cit.,* p. 52.

ple (cf. Num. 15:38 ff.; Deut. 22:11 ff.; Matt. 23:5). This special dress would remind them that they were a special people, dedicated to the service of God. More was involved, however, than the wearing of clothes. With the aping of foreign fashions there came new customs and practices that were offensive to God. This was probably another practice brought in by Manasseh when Assyrian customs infiltrated and permeated the land. This adoption of Assyrian customs led to the acceptance of an alien culture and its religion. The very garments they wore revealed the character of their ideal. They showed little hesitation in surrendering distinctive national characteristics of dress, if by so doing they could gain political and commercial advantages.

It seems that the members of the royal house were the greatest sinners in the area of aping foreign fashions. Certainly they and their court were in the most advantageous position to secure the "latest creations" from the shops of Nineveh, Babylon, and Memphis. However the entire population of Judah was too much in the world and of the world.

h. *Violence and Deceit* (1:9)

I will punish all those that leap over the threshold. Many explanations have been given of the phrase, "leap over the threshold." Some suggest that the reference is to the priests of the god Dagon who avoided walking on the threshold of the temple because his idol had fallen upon it (see I Sam. 5:5). Such a practice then was not only superstitious but was a capitulation to Philistine idolatry. Others suggest that the custom of leaping over the threshold arose from the practice of offering sacrifices to the protecting deities of the house. Since these sacrifices were offered on the threshold, this spot assumed a superstitious sanctity; hence none dared tread upon it. However, careful consideration of the phrase in its context lends weight to the view that the words are expressive of the eagerness and haste with which intruders violated the privacy of homes to rob and to plunder. In their eagerness to pillage the poor they jumped over the threshold of their homes.

that fill their master's house with violence and deceit. Reference is made to the house of the king (master) not to the temple of an idol-deity. Those who placed themselves at the service of the king or his nobles enriched them by committing acts of violence and oppression in their behalf. Both groups would suffer in the coming judgment. "I will punish," saith Jehovah.

2. The Judgment Portrayed (1:7, 14)

Zephaniah pictured the coming universal judgment of God through the use of an expression which was common with the prophets, "the day of Jehovah" (cf. Joel 1:15; Amos 5:18; Obad. 15). This concept was an ancient idea of the prophets (cf. Hos. 4:3; Isa. 2:12) as well as the people (see Amos 5:18), and later prophets only amplified the details of the idea. In general terms the prophets conceived of this day as one in which the Lord would step down into history and make himself known in judgment and/or redemption. One or the other of these elements is often missing from the prophet's message; therefore it is necessary to consider the whole of Old Testament prophecy if an accurate picture of the day is desired. One would not expect the peoples' and the prophets' concept of the day to be identical and the Old Testament verifies this expectation (see, esp. Amos 5:18 ff.). Many Israelites viewed the day as one of joy and gladness for themselves, but a day when God's wrath would be poured out upon all Gentiles. Such an attitude could lead only to carelessness in their devotion toward God and in meeting his moral standards. If judgment were only for the Gentiles, it did not matter how an Israelite lived. So they assumed that they were safe from God's wrath. The prophets repeatedly addressed themselves to correcting this conception of the day of the Lord and warned that it would be a day of gladness or gloom, not on the basis of whether one was Jew or Gentile, but on the basis of whether or not one feared the Lord and served him.

It is clear that Zephaniah's message is largely concerned with "the day of the Lord." He saw it as a time of the destructive outpouring of God's anger upon all men, including particularly the transgressors in Jerusalem and Judah, but also the haughty foreign nations who had oppressed the citizens of the southern kingdom (Judah). H. Ray Dunning has aptly written of Zephaniah: "His central message may be summed up in the phrase, *the day of the Lord is at hand.* This is the day when God will manifest himself as Judge. It is not just any day of calamity, but a special time, the full and final manifestation of God."[5]

vs. 7. *Hold thy peace at the presence of the Lord.* The day of Jehovah does not come apart from the presence of Jehovah himself, in whose presence man had best be silent. Zephaniah vividly realized this presence and shouted for all men to "hush," lest their irreverence bring an even more awesome judgment upon them.

Jehovah hath prepared a sacrifice, he hath consecrated his guests. The day is presented under the symbolism of a great sacrificial meal. Jehovah has made ready the sacrifice (Judah), and the guests who are to share in the sacrificial meal have been consecrated (sanctified). Judah's destruction is so certain that it is seen as already accomplished. Those consecrated are the foes who will devour Judah, and though the prophet does not identify them he probably had in mind the Scythians. It matters not that the Babylonians rather than the Scythians were the eventual destroyers of Judah. The prophet's emphasis was upon the actuality of the day, not the agent of the destruction.

vs. 14. *The great day of Jehovah is near, it is near and hasteth, greatly, even the voice of the day of Jehovah.* This verse is somewhat more advanced and intense than verse 7. As Zephaniah contemplated the day, it assumed amazing proportions fitly described as "great." Its occurrence seemed more imminent. The day was so near that the sound ("voice") of it could be heard. This presentment of its nearness was doubtless intensified by some severe visitation of providence (cf. Joel 1) or by some conclusive movement among the nations. Perhaps with Zephaniah it came as he observed the menacing moves of the Scythians. The prophet however was more concerned with the crisis than with the chronology of its happening.

the mighty man crieth there bitterly. Something of the horror and desolation resulting from God's judgment is pictured in these words. In spite of the din of battle and the dark-

---

[5]*The Minor Prophets,* "Beacon Bible Commentary," Vol. V. (Kansas City: Beacon Hill Press, 1966), p. 301.

ness and desolation of the natural order, all of which accompanies Jehovah's coming, at last when his hand of judgment is lowered, all is quiet. Not a sound is heard save the abject cry of a bloody and baffled warrior, unable either to fight or flee. "There" does not carry the sense of location or place, but *in that day*, that is, the day of Jehovah.

Charles L. Taylor has pointed out that a simple rearrangement of letters in the Massoretic text of a portion of this verse (14) changes it to a much clearer rendering and that without doing violence to the original:[6] "The voice of the day of Jehovah; the mighty man crieth there bitterly" reads, "Swifter than a runner, the day of the Lord, and speedier than a warrior."

3. The Judgment Described (1:15-18, 10-11)

The day of the Lord will be a day of wrath. Zephaniah employs one calamitous figure after another to describe its awesomeness: desolation, darkness, and an assault upon the very walls of the city (Jerusalem) itself. The language of terror is here exhausted. Mixed with the wrath of heaven is the din and stench of war. Blood is as common and worthless as the dust of the ground and human flesh is of no more worth than "dung." All men will be utterly unable to escape, and hoarded wealth will avail them nothing. The day of Jehovah is at hand. And all of this is because men have "sinned against Jehovah."

vs. 15. With this verse Zephaniah begins his vivid description of the horrors of the day of the Lord. The original language is more impressive and awe-inspiring than is possible for any translation to reveal.

That day is a day of wrath. The day of God's judgment is above all a day of *wrath,* of overpowering, crushing wrath. This wrath is God's wrath, poured out upon sinners who have refused to repent. As the effects of the outpouring of divine wrath are detailed, the prophet's description assumed cosmic proportions: *a day of trouble and distress, a day of wasteness and desolation, a day of clouds and thick darkness* (cf. Joel 2:2; Amos 5:20). But these supernatural terrors are not to be regarded as mere figures; for the prophet they were realities. He looked upon

---

[6]*Op. cit.,* p. 1019.

the world as a moral world; therefore, it would be convulsed and dissolved in man's judgment.[7]

The opening words of this verse (15) as they are rendered in the Vulgate version, *Dies irae, dies illa* (day of wrath, that day) are the basis of the most noble of all Latin medieval hymns, the *Dies Irae*. This hymn on the last judgment is attributed to Thomas of Celano (*ca.* 1190-1250), friend and biographer of St. Francis of Assisi, the opening lines of which are:

> O day of wrath, O day of mourning.
> See fulfilled the prophet's warning.
> Heaven and earth is ashes burning.

vs. 16. *a day of the trumpet and alarm, against the fortified cities, and . . . the battlements.* Although the language of the prophet soared to supernatural heights as he described the terrors of the coming judgment, he was too sober and practical to leave the earth completely. Accompanying the terrors from another sphere, indeed a vital part of those horrors were the hostile assaults of enemy forces. The "trumpet" was sounded signaling the approach of the enemy. The war cry ("alarm") of the enemy was heard as he advanced in ever-increasing numbers to execute God's judgment on wicked Judah. "Fortified cities" were no obstacle to his advance; the armed corners ("battlements") of city walls fell into his hands as easily as overripe fruit falls to the ground when the tree is shaken.

vs. 17. *I will bring distress upon men, that they shall walk like blind men.* The distress which was at first outward would lead eventually to inward perplexity when men would grope like the blind. Such a comparison was frequently used to express perplexity and helplessness (cf. Deut. 28:29; Isa. 49:10).

their blood shall be . . . as dust, their flesh as dung. The victors will show their victims no mercy. Flowing blood will be as common and plenteous as the dust of the earth. In utter contempt for human life the conquerors will fling aside the bodies of the slain as so much "dung."

vs. 18. *Neither their silver nor their gold shall . . . deliver them.* Since Jehovah has decreed their punishment bribery will

---

[7]A. B. Davidson, *Nahum, Habakkuk, and Zephaniah,* "The Cambridge Bible for Schools and Colleges," ed. A. F. Kirkpatrick (Cambridge: University Press, 1896), p. 118.

avail them nothing. When will men learn that riches are of little value in times of deepest distress! Could Zephaniah have had in mind the successful efforts of the Egyptians in "buying off" an invasion by the Scythians as reported by Herodotus, the Greek historian?

But the whole land shall be devoured by the fire of his jealousy. Devoured, not delivered, will be the lot of those living when the day of Jehovah comes. The furious fire of God's jealousy (zeal) will consume the "whole land." Some of the versions (cf. RSV) render *earth* for *land,* thus looking upon the judgment as universal (see 1:2).

for he will make an end, yea, a terrible end, of all . . . in the land. It should be emphasized that the day of distress, destruction, and death is the Lord's day. It is his doing; because of the sin of the people (vs. 17) Jehovah has determined to make a sudden ("terrible") end of all that "dwell in the land" (earth).

In verses 15-18 the divine judgment is depicted as primarily universal in scope. In more limited fashion verses 10-11 give a graphic description of what will happen in Jerusalem when the divine invasion occurs. When it comes cries of agony and despair will be heard throughout the city. *There shall be the noise of a cry from the fish gate, and a wailing from the second quarter, and a great crashing from the hills* (vs. 10). The "fish gate" was located in the north wall of the city and was thus named because men from Tyre who traded in dried fish brought them to market by the wall near this gate. "Second quarter" refers to a suburb that had been recently added to the old section of the city — also on the north side, the direction from which invaders would come into the city. The "hills" were either those around Jerusalem in general or more likely reference is to a section of the city by that name. *Wail, ye inhabitants of Maktesh; for all the people of Canaan are undone; all that were laden* (weigh out) *with silver are cut off* (vs. 11). "Maktesh" was probably the hollow between the eastern and western hills on the outskirts of Jerusalem. Its literal meaning is "the mortar" but in Judges 15:19 it is translated "hollow place." This locality was mentioned because it was the place of traders and liable to invasion by any foe from the north, and also because its name portended the coming fate of its occupants.

They would be pounded by their foes (mortar-pounding place). "People of Canaan" is equivalent to *merchant people* since the Canaanites (Phoenicians) were the chief traders in Palestine, and in common usage the term denoted a merchant.[8] Taken together these various locations included at least the major portion of Jerusalem's business life — its markets and its merchantry. Zephaniah strikingly portrayed the sudden howls of pain and anguish from these groups when faced with the certain judgment of God.

The strong imagery of this section should make us consider anew the certainty and seriousness of the judgment of God. God's word is plain at this point. Men cannot continue to fly in the face of God. Man's sin is against God's moral laws and against his holiness. If unforgiven it must be punished. Directed primarily to preachers S. L. Edgar has written: "Fear that we may be classed with those melodramatic preachers who delight to portray the torments of the damned to frighten men into the kingdom has made us too easily forget this whole dimension of biblical teaching."[9] It is a commentary on our society that "pulpit" and "pew" are largely indifferent to the Biblical doctrine of judgment.

4. An Exhortation to Repentance (2:1-3)

Numerous questions have been raised concerning these verses: Are they original with Zephaniah? To what nation do verses 1-2 refer? Are the words of verses 1-2 and verse 3 addressed to citizens of the same nation? In addition, the condition of the text itself is somewhat confused, and its meaning difficult to ascertain. In regard to the first question, the argument has been advanced that the tone of this section is too different from the general tone of the entire book to be from the prophet Zephaniah. But is not the idea of these verses necessary to complete the thought of Chapter 1? The prophets ordinarily did not conclude their words on a note of judgment. For the prophet the usual purpose of judgment was to discipline and hence to purify. It has been suggested further that use of "meek," and

---

[8]H. Ray Dunning, *op. cit.*, p. 303.
[9]*The Minor Prophets*, "Epworth Preacher's Commentaries" (London: The Epworth Press, 1962), pp. 12 f.

"meekness" as religious terms is indicative of an age later than the time of Zephaniah. "But unquestionably the idea that humility before God is the right attitude of men is one of the oldest ideas in Scripture (Ex. :3, J) and one of the most frequently insisted on by the prophets (Is. ii, 11; Mic. vi. 8)."[10] The remaining questions (above) will be clarified (somewhat?) in the exposition of the verses involved.

vs. 1. *Gather yourselves together . . . O nation that has no shame.* The verb used is from the noun *kash* — stubble, straw, chaff, and denotes "to gather stubble" (cf. Exod. 5:7, 12). The verb form used has the causative reflexive sense, that is, to make or cause oneself to stoop. This word is not used in the sense of people gathering or assembling themselves. In every usage the idea of stooping to gather up an object from the ground, to gather by backbreaking work is indicated.[11] Hence the rendering, "Cause yourselves to stoop, yea, stoop . . ." is more nearly correct. The nation called upon to "stoop" was Judah, in spite of the efforts of some[12] to identify it as Philistia (see vs. 4). Verse 3 as well as the indications of Chapter 1 seems to preclude reference to any nation other than Judah. The Hebrew word for nation (*goi*) is the one used of a Gentile nation that does not know God. Proud and haughty Judah had sunk to the level of heathendom. The root *kasaph*, here translated "shame" has the meaning, "to be unabashed" in Aramaic. As applied to Judah the nation had no consciousness of guilt, no humiliation because of sins committed or deeds done, hence no shame.

vs. 2. This verse is admittedly difficult. A. B. Davidson wrote of it, "The verse is probably in some disorder: the first two clauses can hardly present the original text, and the last two clauses look like duplicates."[13] The intent or thrust of the verse is however surprisingly clear: the urgent need of repentance before the coming of the day of Jehovah.

Before the decree bring forth. The reference is to God's decree of judgment which was swiftly moving to its enactment. Before it "brings forth," that is, gives birth to its effects or produces

---

[10]A. B. Davidson, *op. cit.*, p. 101.
[11]Theodore Laetsch, *op. cit.*, p. 365.
[12]Charles L. Taylor, *op. cit.*, p. 1021.
[13]*Op cit.*, p. 120.

its fruit of destruction, Zephaniah exhorts the haughty nation to "stoop" in true humility before the covenant God.

before the day pass as the chaff. More literally, "As chaff he passed on (the) day." "Before" is missing in the original. Contrary to the translation of the Septuagint, "Before you become like drifting chaff," the intent of the Hebrew is not to draw a parallel between chaff carried away by the wind, or swiftly consumed by the fire, and the fate of the people of Jerusalem. Rather, the emphasis is upon the swift approach of the day of Jehovah, the day of judgment. Since this day was approaching as swiftly as chaff blown by the wind, the prophet exhorted the people to repent swiftly before it was too late, before "the fierce anger of Jehovah . . . before the day of Jehovah's anger come upon you."

vs. 3. Whereas the exhortation of the two previous verses was directed at the haughty, self-exalting ones of Judah, this verse concerns itself with the faithful few, as Zephaniah in softer tones encouraged them not to despair of God's protection even in face of the coming calamity. If they "seek Jehovah" they will escape his wrath.

all ye meek of the earth, that have kept his ordinances. The "meek" are those who are opposite in character to the proud, self-sufficient, and shameless previously addressed (v. 1). This characterization was wider than class distinctions. The humble among both rich and poor were included. Though this exhortation to seek the Lord was addressed primarily to the people of Judah, there is no necessity for the rendering "meek of the *land.*" The Hebrew (*haaretz*) is variously translated "the earth" or "the land." The meek are further described as those who had kept the ordinances of Jehovah; who had acted in accordance with his revealed will in keeping themselves from the sins denounced above (chap. 1); those who had made the norm of God's law the sole rule of their lives.

seek righteousness, seek meekness. It is significant to observe that seeking righteousness and meekness is equated in this verse with seeking God. In actuality righteousness (right according to God's standard) and meekness (humility in action) are the practical fruits of God-seeking, and meet two of God's three requirements of the Old Testament saint: "And what does Jehovah require of thee, but to do justly [right] . . . and to walk humbly with thy God" (Micah 6:8b-c). G. A. Smith had discerningly called attention to the absence of all mention of divine mercy as the cause of deliverance. "Zephaniah has no gospel of that kind. The conditions of escape are sternly ethical — meekness, the doing of justice and righteousness."[14]

it may be ye will be hid in the day of Jehovah's anger. Better, "perhaps you will be hid," an expression of humble but confident petition. Zephaniah could go no further; it must remain for one with a more sensitive heart, with less austerity to take the final leap of faith to an absolute confidence in the "hiding-power" of God.

Dunning has called attention to the fact that in 1:15–2:3 Zephaniah presents his picture of "The Great Day of Jehovah." On one side of the picture there is the heavy hand of God's justice which brings terror, wrath, and destruction upon those who flagrantly sin against him. On the other side there is the high hope of God's mercy which encourages every man to seek him in meekness, obedience, and righteousness.[15]

C. JUDGMENT ON THE NATIONS (2:4-15)

In this section Zephaniah predicts destruction for some of the nations which were long-time enemies of Israel. Although all of her enemies are not included, it seems reasonable to assume that the prophet meant for those denounced to be representative of the larger group. In Zephaniah's eyes all who opposed the Lord or his people were under his judgment. The nations on which God's judgment was to fall were Philistia, Moab and Ammon, Ethiopia, and Assyria. With respect to Judah the four nations (Moab and Ammon are denounced as one) lay respectively west, east, south, and north. Two of them are far, Ethiopia and Assyria, and two are near, Philistia and Moab-Ammon. Thus the element of universality is introduced as far and near are combined with all the points of the compass. Zephaniah unlike Amos (cf. Amos 1:3–2:3) did not announce in every case the specific sin(s) with which the nation was charged, thus vindi-

---

[14]*Op. cit.*, p. 58.
[15]*Op. cit.*, p. 306.

cating Jehovah's justice. Apparently the former was primarily concerned with Judah, and here he left no doubts as to the moral demands of God. For Zephaniah Jehovah needed no vindication; he and he alone was the sovereign Lord of the universe.

1. Judgment on Philistia (2:4-7)

The Philistines lived on the fertile plains in a south-westerly direction from Jerusalem and their land was bordered on the west by the Mediterranean Sea. Four of their five chief cities are mentioned by Zephaniah: Gaza, Ashkelon, Ashdod, and Ekron. Gath is omitted, perhaps because it was left in ruins following its conquest by Assyria.

For Gaza shall be forsaken, and Ashkelon a desolation. The conjunction "for" either connects this entire section (4-15) with the world-wide judgment declared in the first chapter, or it refers to the injunction in verse 3, "Seek ye Jehovah . . . it may be ye will be hid," for many will be destroyed. For the most part the prophet used common terms of destruction to indicate the fate of these Philistine cities: "forsaken" and "desolation," both of which words carry the sense of depopulated. There is perhaps a pun or play on words as regards Gaza (*azzah*) and "forsaken" (*azubah*).

they shall drive out Ashdod at noonday and Ekron shall be rooted up. The idea involved in the phrase "at noonday" is not entirely clear. Perhaps it suggests the ease with which the city will fall, that is, the attack will last only until noonday. Or again, this city will appear so weak and defenseless to its invader that they need not attempt to take it by surprise (at night), but by an open attack (at noon). Less likely is the explanation that the attack upon the city would be made at noonday, when the populace was accustomed to lounging, and hence would be unprepared to defend themselves. Another play on words is found with Ekron (*'eqron*) and "rooted up" (*'aqer*).

vs. 5. *Woe unto the inhabitants of the sea-coast, the nation of the Cherethites.* Zephaniah next announced "woe" upon the "inhabitants of the sea-coast," that is, the Philistines, who had lived along the Mediterranean Sea since *ca.* 1200 B.C., following their migration from Asia Minor and the Mediterranean area, including the island of Crete. (Cf. Amos 9:7, "Have not I brought up . . . the Philistines from Caphtor [Crete]?") "Chere-thites," here another name for Philistines, are believed to have inhabited the southern part of the Philistine sea-coast (see I Sam. 30:14; Ezek. 25:16). The name is doubtlessly connected with their association (origin) with the island of Crete.

The word of Jehovah is against you, O Canaan, the land of the Philistines. The use of Canaan as synonymous with "land of the Philistines" is found only here in the Old Testament. Such usage has occasioned some difficulty, but according to Joshua (13:3 f.) the territory of the Philistines was "reckoned to the Canaanites." Some delete the word (Canaan) or at best, consider it out of place in the text. Others look upon it as more than the designation of a district and consider it as the description of a greedy commercialism which was characteristic of the Canaanites (cf. its use in 1:11). In any case the weighty word of Jehovah's judgment is upon the Philistines. Their land will soon be without inhabitant and stripped of its glory.

vs. 6. *And the sea-coast shall be pastures, with cottages for shepherds and folds for flocks.* Whatever difficulties others may have with the text of this verse, its sense or meaning is clear: the cities of the Philistines will be depopulated and desolate, the entire territory will be fit only for pastures.

vs. 7. Many critics consider the whole of this verse a later addition since it introduces a new note in the prophecy, the eventual return of the Israelites from exile, and since in Zephaniah's day they had not as yet experienced exile. This is not a sufficient reason for denying the prophecy to Zephaniah. For while the verse does indicate that the "remnant of the house of Judah" will feed their flocks from the territory now possessed by the Philistines, and that this same remnant will rest themselves in the "houses of Ashkelon," the time is not necessarily after the Exile. Such a conclusion is derived only from an incorrect interpretation of the latter part of this verse, "for Jehovah their God will visit them, and bring back their captivity," or "turn away their captivity" (KJV). The expression is better rendered, "restore their prosperity," or "return their fortunes (cf. Job 42:10; Hos. 6:11; Amos 9:14).

Zephaniah had already envisoned the possibility of a remnant of Judah surviving the day of Jehovah (see 2:3). Now he is concerned with the judgment of Philistia in that same great day. What could have been more natural and logical than for him to have seen as part of God's punishment upon the Philistines loss of their lands to the "remnant of Judah"? But, and this is the point of emphasis, the remnant does not necessarily have to be a remnant from the exiled of Judah. This writer has no objection to its being such a remnant, nor to the prophet's being able to foresee it, but this does not appear to be the meaning here.

2. Judgment on Moab and Ammon (2:8-11)

Moab was the high, level plateau bordering the east banks of the Dead Sea. Ammon was located east of Jericho, across the Jordan River and to the north of Moab. They are denounced as one because both lay along the eastern border of Israel. The Moabites and Ammonites, descendants of Lot (see Gen. 19:30-38), were unrelenting enemies of the Israelites, although they were related by blood. Zephaniah is more explicit about the sins of these peoples than any others he denounced (except his own, Judah). Note that the speaker is God himself.

vs. 8. *I have heard the reproach of Moab and the revelings of the children of Ammon.* The sin for which these ancient enemies of Israel were called into account was that of abusive speech or offensive design expressed in arrogant words (cf. Jer. 48:27-29; Isa. 16:6; Ezek. 21:28; 25:3, 6, 8). The object of their boastings and derisive scorn was Israel. Hence their disdainful boastings were also against Jehovah. The literal meaning of *magnified themselves against their border is,* "They enlarged their mouths concerning their border," that is, they boasted they would annex land belonging to Israel.

Therefore as I live, saith Jehovah. . . . Surely Moab shall be as Sodom and . . . Ammon as Gomorrah. In seeking to vaunt themselves over God's people and in attempting to take their land, Moab and Ammon had rebelled against *Jehovah of hosts, the God of Israel.* Their punishment, therefore, was certain; doubly certain for Jehovah had sworn or taken an oath — the strongest possible oath — he had sworn by himself, "As surely as I live, saith Jehovah of hosts." Use of the name, "Jehovah of hosts," indicates that sufficient strength and power were available for him to make effective his threats against the enemies of his people. Israel's God is in command of innumerable hosts of spiritual and material forces. He is indeed omnipotent, Lord of the armies (hosts) of heaven. The utter destruction of Sodom and Gomorrah is proverbial in the Bible (cf. Deut. 29:22 ff.; Isa. 13:19). A further reason for reference to these two cities may be found in their relation to the ancestors of the Moabites and Ammonites (see Gen. 19).

a possession of nettles, and saltpits. A further description of the "perpetual desolation" which will befall Moab and Ammon. Their land will become a place fit only for the growing of "nettles," a type of plant which grows only in uncultivated, waste places. In locations where salt is plentiful, as the Dead Sea area, the soil is barren and desolate for little if any vegetation can grow.

the residue of my people shall make a prey of them and the remnant of my nation shall inherit them. Moab's and Ammon's loss will be total and complete: their lands will be made desolate by Jehovah of hosts and their nations plundered and absorbed by his people. "Residue" and "remnant" do not necessarily mean returnees from the Exile (see exposition of verse 7).

vs. 10. *This shall they have for their pride.* The peoples of Moab and Ammon had paraded their arrogance before the Israelites. In so doing they had shown their insolence toward Israel's God; now their pride would be reduced to utter humility through calamities sent upon them by this selfsame God.

vs. 11. *Jehovah will . . . famish all the gods of the earth.* "Famish" means *to make lean, to diminish.* Zephaniah was looking forward to the time when God would cause all gods of the earth to disappear. How he is to do this is not exactly clear. Perhaps, as Jehovah is to be "terrible" unto Moab and Ammon just so will he be to all other nations, thus stripping them of their inhabitants who can then no longer feed their gods sacrifices. Thus the gods will come lean and eventually diminish or disappear. Others suggest that Jehovah will make himself known by his great and terrible deeds. Then the inhabitants of other nations will follow Jehovah, forsaking their gods and leaving them to "famish."

and men shall worship him, every one from his place. When all other gods have been found impotent, then all men will turn to Jehovah the true and living God and worship him "every one from his place," that is, each in his own place. Pilgrimages to Jerusalem will be no longer necessary. This speaks of the universal worship of Jehovah, "even all the isles [coastlands] of the nations." The time? What matters the time, glory in the truth!

3. Judgment on Ethiopia (2:12)

It is possible that this verse is only a fragment of a more complete oracle delivered by Zephaniah against the "Ethiopians," Hebrew *Kushim*, "Cushites" or inhabitants of Cush. *Kush* included Nubia and parts of Arabia bordering on the Red Sea. Also, it is possible that this verse refers to Egypt which is called Ethiopia only because of her subjection to Ethiopic dynasties.

Ye Ethiopians also, ye shall be slain by my sword. "Also," that is, like Philisitia, Moab, and Ammon, Ethiopia is to feel the onslaught of an invader. "My sword," the Lord's sword is whatever instrument he uses to effect his purpose of punishment (cf. Isa. 34:5; Ezek. 30:25). No further details are given. Since Ethiopia was neither an immediate neighbor nor an enemy of Israel, a possible purpose of this brief oracle was to show the universal scope of Jehovah's sovereignty.

4. Judgment on Assyria (2:13-15)

Whether planned, or otherwise, the climax of Zephaniah's denunciation of the nations was reached with Assyria, colossus of the ancient world whose empire was beginning to crumble in Zephaniah's time.

vs. 13. *And he will stretch out his hand against the north, and destroy Assyria, and . . . make Nineveh a desolation.* Jehovah "will stretch out his hand" in order to smite. The one to be smitten is from the north, obviously Assyria whose capital city, Nineveh, lay some five hundred miles to the northeast of Judah, but whose armies would have to cross the Euphrates River at the city of Carchemish, approximately three hundred miles west of Nineveh, and thus would enter Palestine from the north. This nation which had dominated the world for almost five hundred years (1100-612 B.C.) will be destroyed; her capital city as barren and desolate as a dry wilderness.

vs. 14. *And herds shall lie down in the midst of her, all the beasts of the nations.* As further evidence of the complete desolation of Nineveh, Zephaniah gives a detailed description of conditions in the city as the result of God's smiting. In graphic language he pictures the absence of human inhabitants in the desolate ruins of the doomed capital. "Herds" (flocks) lie down in the very midst of the once inhabited city. It has become a lair for wild beats "of the nations," better translated, "of all kinds."

the pelican and the porcupine shall lodge in the capitals. The "capitals" were the carved tops of the supporting pillars of a building. Pelicans will roost on those pillars still standing among the ruins; while porcupines will make their dens in those which have fallen to the ground. (Some substitute vulture for pelican and hedgehog for porcupine.)

their voice shall sing in the window. "Their" is not in the original. The "voice" is either the sighing, moaning sound of the wind blowing through the vacant windows or the song of birds who now inhabit the vacant ruins.

desolation shall be in the thresholds. Like a grim specter desolation and ruin occupy the debris-cluttered thresholds of the dwellings of gods and men. Some read "raven" for "desolation."

for he hath laid bare the cedar-work. The elaborate panelings covering the walls and ceilings have been laid bare (by Jehovah) leaving them exposed to the ravages of wind and rain.

What a picture of destruction, desolation, death! The great city which once had reveled in luxury and wealth has become a home for flocks and herds and a haunt for wild animals, her ancient and once impregnable glory reduced to ruins akin to those with which she had littered the centuries.

vs. 15. *This is the joyous city that dwelt carelessly, that said in her heart, I am, and . . . none besides me.* Assuming the role for a moment of a former victim of Assyrian cruelty and oppression, Zephaniah looked contemptuously at the ruins of the once proud city and taunted with exultation. In the words of the taunt the true cause of Nineveh's downfall is found. In the first place she "dwelt carelessly," she felt quite secure for she assumed there were no rivals to question her supremacy. Such careless living was based upon a false confidence in temporal power and an imagined security against both poverty and national destruction. Also, in her pride she arrogated to herself an attribute reserved only for Deity: "I am, and there is none besides me," had been her challenge to Israel, to the world, yea, even to Jehovah himself. This challenge did not go unanswered, and the boastful city passed through the portals of oblivion.

how is she become a desolation, a place for beasts to lie down. These words are either an explanation or an exclamation. If the former they point to the first part of the verse as the explanation or reason for Nineveh's utter desolation. If they are exclamatory then the sense is, "What a desolation she has become, a place fit only for animals to live!"

every one that passeth by her shall hiss, and wag his hand. The pent-up feelings of Nineveh's enemies, after long seething under the Assyrian yoke, finally burst forth in full fury and unrestrained emotion. The first expression, "shall hiss," is indicative of scorn and detestation; the second, "wag his hand," is a gesture of defiance and hatred, similar to our "shake the fist at."

The utter destruction of the Assyrian capital is a fact of history. Nineveh was so completely destroyed that its very location was lost to the memory of man until the nineteenth century when it was discovered by archaeologists.

D. JUDGMENT REAFFIRMED (3:1-8)

H. L. Ellison[16] is probably correct in his view that we find in this section the explanation of why in 1:2—2:3 social sin and wrongdoing are scarcely mentioned. However perverted and grievous the corrupt worship of Jerusalem, for Zephaniah the social injustice was infinitely worse. For him, as for all the prophets, social unrighteousness was the apex of iniquity, the supreme sin, the one unanswerable indictment of the people's corrupt worship of God. Therefore, these sins are dealt with as the climax of his prophecies of judgment.

1. On Jerusalem (3:1-7)

The prophet again turns his attention to Jerusalem (cf. 1:4-13). He denounces particularly the oppression and moral ob-

---

[16]*Op. cit.*, p. 68.

stinacy which was characteristic of all classes of society. Though he does not name the object of his reproof, it is obviously Jerusalem.

vs. 1. *Woe to her that is rebellious and polluted! to the oppressing city.* The prophet's first word is one of "woe" upon Jerusalem, characterized as "rebellious," "polluted," and "oppressing." All three characteristics are dealt with further in the following verses. "Polluted" is a term usually connected with blood (cf. Isa. 59:3; Lam. 4:14).

vs. 2. This verse for the most part expands Zephaniah's charge of rebelliousness brought forward in verse 1. The city's perversity is seen in the following accusations: (1) *she obeyed not the voice,* that is, the voice of God as communicated through his prophets; (2) *she received not correction,* that is, God's repeated warnings to her by his spokesmen went unheeded, as did his judgments upon surrounding nations; (3) *she trusted not in Jehovah,* as evidenced by seeking security in foreign alliances; and (4) *she drew not near to her God,* but sought after other gods (*baalim*) of the land. In all four of these accusations the word order of the original is significant. In the first two the negative particle (not) receives the emphatic position: "*Not* she has obeyed" (heard), "*Not* she has received." In the other two the name of God receives the primary position of emphasis followed by the negative: "*In Jehovah* not she trusted," "*Unto her God* [Elohim] not she drew near."

vss. 3-4. In these two verses Zephaniah denounces both the civil and religious leaders of Jerusalem and characterizes their sins, using the imagery of wild animals as well as more conventional language (cf. Micah 3).

Her princes . . . are roaring lions. Those in authority and power whether members of the royal house or not, had no regard for justice and righteousness. As "roaring lions" when hungry are eager to spring upon their prey, so the leaders of Jerusalem (Judah) went about seeking for victims whom they could devour (cf. Ezek. 25:27).

her judges are evening wolves; they leave nothing till the morning. Judah's judges are compared to "evening wolves" that go in search of food under cover of darkness, and when they find it they gulp down the prey, bones and all, leaving nothing till the morrow. In similar fashion the judges of Jerusalem showed no mercy in their inhuman greed. Under pretense of law and justice they fleeced their victims. Their greed was insatiable, they were always hungry for more gain.

Her prophets are light and treacherous persons. Judah's spiritual leaders also had failed in their function. Her prophets were "light," that is, frivolous, unstable. They had a low view of their vocation and could not be trusted for they proclaimed the imaginations of their own minds as true revelations from God.

her priests have profaned the sanctuary, they have done violence to the law. The word "sanctuary" is better translated *sacred* or *holy.* Judah's priests then had profaned the sacred or holy. One of the priest's prime functions was to act as a guardian of holiness in order to insure the proper conditions for the meeting of God and man in worship. The priests of Judah had become worldly-minded, and no longer made a distinction between the profane and the holy (cf. Ezek. 22:26). These same priests did "violence to the law" as they twisted it to suit their own advantage, to fill their own paunches and purses.

vs. 5. As if to give further evidence of their rebelliousness and stubbornness (see vss. 1, 2) the prophet points out that even the presence and operations of the righteous Lord in their midst had not deterred or instructed those who practiced the evils described (vss. 3-4). Nevertheless his abiding presence made their conduct all the more reprehensible, their judgment more certain and serious.

every morning doth he bring his justice to light, he faileth not. Jehovah constantly brings his judgment or justice to light. It is visible to all except those who are determined not to see. His moral rule, his standards of righteousness are as constant and visible to men as the natural law that ushers in the dawn. But Judah refuses to see and to heed.

but the unjust knoweth no shame. Nothing seems to have moved the calloused citizens of Jerusalem, not even the consistently clear evidence of God's moral government in their midst. Unmoved by the righteousness of God and impervious to any instruction from his righteous rule, they stubbornly pursued their own satisfactions with no sense of shame.

vs. 6. The thought of the preceding verse is continued: Jehovah's righteous rule is exercised not alone within Judah but also among the nations without. These judgments were also meant for Judah's instruction but she willfully refused to hear.

I have cut off nations . . . so that there is no inhabitant. Note that the speaker is God not the prophet. This change adds emphasis to what is said. Nations have been "cut off" (by God); they are now in desolation and ruin, without "inhabitants." No particular nation is named but history was already replete with examples of nations (peoples) who rose to heights of glory and power, then because of sin suffered decline and disintegration — at God's hand, "I have cut off." Surely the Northern Kingdom (Israel) must have been one of the nations to which the prophet referred. Zephaniah sees God's purpose in his judgments on the nations as a warning to Judah, that she might receive instruction from them, but she was adamant to correction (instruction) and became increasingly corrupt.

vs. 7. *I said, Only fear thou me, receive correction.* God is still the speaker (cf. vs. 6). "I said" in the sense of "I thought." Read, "Only fear thou me" as "Surely thou wilt fear me." God had hoped (thought) that the many examples of his justice and righteousness (see vss. 5-6) would have an effect upon Judah such as would lead her to "receive correction" from him. Had she done so, then it would not have been necessary for God to *cut off her dwelling,* "howsoever he punished her" otherwise. (This last clause is perhaps a more understandable rendering of the difficult "according to all that I have appointed concerning her.")

but they rose early and corrupted all their doings. God's hopes for Judah were never realized. His warnings to Jerusalem which should have made the citizens examine themselves and return to God, made them more rebellious than before, resulting in an eagerness on their part to make their deeds even more corrupt. "Rose early" is a Hebrew idiom meaning to do something eagerly or earnestly.

2. On the Nations (3:8)

To this point in the third chapter Zephaniah has focused his attention exclusively on the rebellion of Jerusalem, the character of her leaders, and her stubborn refusal to be instructed with reference to God's judgment on conquered cities of neighboring nations. He has uttered no word with reference to the major theme of the book, the day of Jehovah. But now, in a transitional verse, the voice of the Lord is heard declaring the approach of that decisive day on which he has purposed to gather the nations to pour out his righteous wrath upon them.

Therefore wait ye for me, saith Jehovah, until the day that I rise up to the prey. The identity of those exhorted or invited "to wait" is somewhat uncertain. Is reference made to the "meek" of Jerusalem (cf. 2:3) or to believers everywhere? It can hardly be an invitation to the prophet himself to await God's execution of his purpose of judgment upon all peoples for a plural subject is addressed. It seems, rather, an invitation to Jehovah's loyal adherents wherever they may be, to await patiently his destructive deeds in the hope of escape and blessing. The "prey" is the nations to be destroyed; in the Septuagint, "witness," with the meaning that God would rise up and witness against the nations faced with destruction. "Therefore" connects this verse with verses 1-7; since the sinners of Jerusalem have willfully refused to receive "correction" from Jehovah, divine chastisement is certain.

my determination is to gather the nations . . . assemble the kingdoms, to pour upon them . . . my fierce anger. The "nations" have been found guilty in Jehovah's court of justice. It remains only for the righteous Judge to execute the "determination," literally, *judgment.* "To gather the nations" does not mean that Jerusalem will be the gathering place; rather the idea is expressed that they will be simultaneously and universally judged: *for all the earth shall be devoured with the fire of my jealousy.* Judgment must surge once again over the nations and over Judah at the hand of the only one who has the right to inflict it — Jehovah.

II. THE UNLIMITED REDEMPTION (DELIVERANCE) OF GOD (3:9-20)

A. THE PROMISE OF REDEMPTION (CONVERSION) (3:9-13)

These verses describe a day when, as the results of the disciplinary judgments of God, there will be a world-wide conversion or turning of peoples to Jehovah. With God judgment is not an end within itself. He does not punish arbitrarily, just because he is God and has the power to punish. And as his judgments are always just, so too are they always linked, explicitly or implicitly, with redemption and restoration. They are never purely punitive, but have as their final purpose blessing. Zephaniah has clearly indicated that God's judgment would be universal (see 1:2-3; 2:4-15), now it is his purpose to describe the universal blessings which will result from that judgment. This section of Zephaniah's prophecies is like the quiet calm after a surging storm. After God's judgments have worked their work, he will graciously bring all the nations and Israel to a true knowledge of himself.

1. To the Heathen (3:9-10)

For then will I turn to the peoples a pure language. "For then" not only relates this verse to the previous one chronologically, that is, after the great judgment described in verse 8, but it also states another reason for patient, hopeful trust in the Lord (cf. 2:3; 3:8a). The verb "turn" is used in the sense of changing the nature of an object, for example, "God gave him another heart" (I Sam. 10:9). That is, God turned Saul's heart into another heart. "Pure language" is more literally *purified lip* (Heb.). Jehovah, following his universal judgment, will change the impure lip of the peoples to a pure one. Though the lips of the peoples were contaminated by the mention of idolatrous gods, the cleansing indicated is deeper than the lips. In the Temple Isaiah cried out, "I am a man of unclean lips"

(Isa. 6:5), to which God responded, "Thine iniquity is taken away, and thy sin forgiven" (6:7). The lip (speech) is symbolic of an inner condition. Here then is a promise of a purified heart which results in a purified language. It is not indicated how this divine work is to be accomplished, but it is clear that it is the work of God.

that they may call upon the name of Jehovah, to serve him with one consent. The "purified lip" (new heart) is given not that they *may* call upon Jehovah, not that they *may* serve him unitedly; but rather, as the result of the change wrought by him, they will worship ("call upon") him in an acceptable fashion and serve him "with one consent," literally one *shoulder.* This is a figure borrowed from farming. When several oxen were working together they were joined by a single yoke; they worked as one. Hence the rendering in the Septuagint, "to serve him under one yoke." The nations of the world will worship Jehovah with such zeal and unity that it will be as the worship of one (nation).

vs. 10. *From beyond the rivers of Ethiopia.* That is, from the uttermost part of the earth (known world). On Ethiopia or Cush see exposition of 2:12.

my suppliants, even the daughter of my dispersed, shall bring mine offering. This portion of vs. 10 is difficult. Two interpretations are possible: (1) The exiled Israelites ("my suppliants, even the daughter of my dispersed") will return bringing to Jehovah sacrifices of thanksgiving for their deliverance; and (2) the heathen nations, in whose lands the dispersed Israelites are living, will bring them back to their own soil as an offering to God, thus giving proof of their own conversion by releasing the captive Israelites (cf. Isa. 66:20). The latter interpretation seems preferable, particularly in context with vs. 9. There attention is called to the conversion of the nations to the true worship of Jehovah. What better practical proof of their conversion could these nations offer than to return captives to their homeland as free men. Furthermore, the return (conversion) of the Israelites is rather clearly taken up in the next verse (11), rather than this one (10). In regard to the idea of universal salvation found in this passage, the teaching is not uncommon in the Old Testament (cf. esp. Isa. 2:2-4; Micah 4:1-4; Isa. 11:9; 19:23-25; 49:5-6).

2. To a Remnant of Israel (3:11-13)

These verses are doubtlessly addressed to the city of Jerusalem, but are directed to an humble, upright, and cleansed remnant who will be gathered there, where they will find refuge and live without fear.

vs. 11. *In that day shalt thou not be put to shame for all thy doings.* "In that day" refers to the general period spoken of in the context of these verses, that is, the day when the nations have been purified by the fires of Divine judgment and the people of God cleansed and converted. To be "put to shame" means either to bear as a burden the shame of, or to feel the sense of shame for, past deeds or "doings." The latter sense is preferable, but in either case past "transgressions" (rebellions) are so completely removed by God that they no longer result in a blush or a burden of shame. How this removal is accomplished is not indicated, but 'tis done. Hallelujah!

I will take away . . . thy proudly exulting ones. A further reason for the lack of shame in Jerusalem is the fact that God will remove the "proudly exulting ones" by the fires of his judgment. The proud ones are primarily princes, judges, prophets, and priests who have flagrantly sinned in violation of the plainest laws (cf. 3:3 f.). But Jehovah will take them away, and haughtiness will no more be found on his "holy mountain" in Jerusalem.

vs. 12. *I will leave in the midst of thee an afflicted and poor people.* Out of the judgment of the day of Jehovah, indeed because of its refining fires, there will remain those in Jerusalem described as "afflicted and poor." The word "afflicted" hardly carries any of its modern meaning, e.g., *dire distress,* but is the opposite of powerful or haughty, that is, *lowly, meek.* The city of Zion will be populated with a humble, upright, and honest remnant instead of a proud and rebellious people (cf. 3:1-5). This lowly and poor people left in Zion will be characterized by an humble trust ("take refuge") in "the name of Jehovah!" Since Jehovah's name stands for the revealed nature of his innermost being, to trust in his name is equivalent to trusting in him.

vs. 13. *The remnant of Israel shall not do iniquity, nor speak lies; neither shall a deceitful tongue be found.* The "remnant" referred to is the group who will "take refuge" (trust) in Jehovah's name (see vs. 12). They are the cleansed ones who will remain in the land after all sinners have been consumed. They will become like the God whom they worship; therefore they will do no "iniquity" (see 3:5). Iniquity = *perverseness, crookedness.* Neither will there be found among them the sins of lying and deceit.

for they shall feed and lie down, and none shall make them afraid. This figure of flocks feeding and lying down unafraid gives a perfect picture of complete security and is a common one in the Old Testament (cf. Isa. 17:2; Ezek. 34:25, 28). This result accrues only to those who take refuge in Jehovah.

B. A PICTURE OF THE REDEEMED (3:14-20)

Because the tender tone of these verses stands in such radical contrast to the harsh note of the remainder of the prophecy, numerous scholars maintain that this section belongs to post-exilic times. Even if this were an established fact, it, of course, would not be inconsistent with the fullest inspiration of the entire book; but the possibility of its being Zephaniah's authentic word has never been adequately disproved (cf. Intro., pp. 64 f.).

The prophet now anticipates the time when the afflictions of Zion shall be over, when her captive children shall be restored, and when Jehovah's full presence shall be in her midst as Redeemer and King. Surely, all of this is reason for rejoicing: *Sing O daughter of Zion; shout, O Israel . . . rejoice with all the heart, O daughter of Jerusalem* (vs. 14). In a poetical sense, cities with their inhabitants were frequently referred to as women (see Isa. 47:1; Ps. 45:12). "Daughter of Zion" and "daughter of Jerusalem" are parallel to and synonymous with "Israel."

vs. 15. This verse gives the grounds for Judah's rejoicing. The verbs are in the "prophetic perfect"; the events though future are described as having taken place already.

Jehovah hath taken away thy judgments, he hath cast out thine enemy. Judah's "judgments" were the chastisements inflicted upon her because of her iniquity. These are now "taken away" for "her warfare is accomplished . . . her iniquity is pardoned" (cf. Isa. 40:2). God has worked his work of cleansing through judgment; therefore, the nation ("thine enemy") which he had used as the instrument of his judgment would be "cast out."

the King of Israel, even Jehovah, is in the midst of thee; thou shalt not fear evil anymore. Since Israel is now prepared for Jehovah's presence, by the removal of her sins, he *is* present in her midst as Protector; therefore, she need not — yea, she *will not* — "fear evil anymore." Some render, "see evil anymore," that is, experienced it. Jehovah is often called "King of Israel" (cf. Isa. 6:5; 44:6).

vs. 16. *it shall be said to Jerusalem, Fear thou not . . . let not thy hands be slack.* With Jehovah in her midst Jerusalem need not fear nor let her hands fall to her side in helplessness and despair. The presence of the Lord will give confidence in every emergency.

vs. 17. *Jehovah thy God is in the midst of thee, a mighty one who will save.* The basis for Zion's fearlessness is again indicated as the presence of Jehovah in her midst (cf. vs. 15). He is now pictured as "a mighty one," a victorious warrior who is able to effect every needed deliverance.

he will rejoice over thee . . . he will joy over thee. These words aptly portray "the gladness of God" over his work of redemption or deliverance. As he contemplated his people cleansed, unafraid, and living triumphantly for him, his own heart overflowed with the emotion of joy and gladness. It is not surprising that this verse has been called "the most beautiful verse in the entire book." Mutual fellowship between God and his people always results in mutual joys. What a privilege to bring joy to the heart of God!

vs. 18. This verse is difficult and there are various renderings. As further cause for joy on the part of the people of God Jehovah will gather (literally, *hath gathered*) those in exile who cannot enjoy the sacred festivals and seasons (*solemn assembly*) in Jerusalem and whose very absence is a reproach to the city. United and with God's power over all gods vindicated, Israel will live in happiness and without reproach.

vss. 19-20. In addition to further treatment of thoughts previously considered, namely, destruction of Judah's enemies (vs. 15) and gathering of the dispersed of Israel (vs. 18), these verses introduce the idea of the exaltation of the faithful among the nations of the earth. Twice the prophet states that Jehovah will make his people *a name and a praise* among all the peoples of the earth. Whether the meaning is that the people, being righteous and blessed, are consequently the *source* of renown and praise to Jehovah, or that the people themselves are the *object* of praise by all the nations is not clear. In either case there is added cause for joy and rejoicing by those whom God will redeem. This deliverance, or restoration of their former fortunes is imminent; it will come in their lifetime, *before your eyes.* Furthermore, this promised deliverance is certain, assured by the affixed seal of divine authority, *saith Jehovah.*

Thus, in spite of the dark background of universal judgment against which Zephaniah has presented his message, he comes at last to look beyond the day of desolation and destruction to an era when universal homage will be shown Jehovah. For the prophet, God's judgments were always just and always accomplished a beneficent, redeeming purpose. He saw the time coming when those from distant nations would call on the name of the Lord, and when the humble and lowly remnant of Israel would dwell in safety and peace under the righteous rule of Jehovah their King. In that day the people of God would be no longer sinning but singing: "Sing, O daughter of Zion; shout O Israel . . . rejoice with all thy heart, O daughter of Jerusalem" for "Jehovah . . . the King of Israel . . . is in the midst of thee" (3:14 f.).

BIBLIOGRAPHY

Caiger, Stephen L., *Lives of the Prophets*. London: S.P.C.K., 1958.

Calkins, Raymond, *The Modern Message of the Minor Prophets*. New York, Harper and Brothers, 1947.

Carson, J. T., "Zephaniah," *The New Bible Commentary*. London: The InterVarsity Fellowship, 1952.

Davidson, A. B., *Nahum, Nabakkuk and Zephaniah*, "The Cambridge Bible Series." Cambridge: The University Press, 1896.

Driver, S. R., *The Minor Prophets*, "The Century Bible." New York: Oxford University Press, 1906.

Dunning, H. Ray, *The Minor Prophets*, "Beacon Bible Commentary," Vol. V. Kansas City: Beacon Hill Press, 1966.

Edgar, S. L., *The Minor Prophets*, "The Epworth Preacher's Commentaries." London: The Epworth Press, 1962.

Laetsch, Theodore, *The Minor Prophets*, "Bible Commentary." St. Louis: Concordia Publishing House, 1956.

Lehrman, S. M., *The Twelve Prophets*, "The Soncino Books of the Bible." Bournemouth: The Soncino Press, 1948.

Taylor, Charles L. and Thurman, Howard, *The Book of Zephaniah*, "Interpreter's Bible," Vol. VI. Nashville: Abingdon Press, 1956.